Employment Law Checklists

EMPLOYMENT LAW LIBRARY

Employment Law
Checklists

Julia Palca

Series editor: John Bowers, MA, BCL, Barrister

BLACKSTONE
PRESS LIMITED

First published in Great Britain 1993 by Blackstone Press Limited,
9-15 Aldine Street, London W12 8AW. Telephone 081-740 1173

ISBN: 1 85431 212 X

British Library Cataloguing in Publication Data
A CIP catalogue record for this book is available from the British Library.

Typeset by Style Photosetting, Mayfield, East Sussex
Printed by BPCC Wheatons Ltd, Exeter

Contents

Preface

I have written this book with the aim that it will be of assistance to lawyers who do not profess to be experts in employment law and to non-lawyers, such as personnel managers, who deal on a day to day basis with employment and industrial relations issues. The book is intended to be practical, guiding the reader as to the appropriate steps which need to be taken and facts which need to be considered before employment decisions are reached.

Because the book is not intended for the employment law practitioner, I have not included any statute or case references in the book. The book sets out the law as it stood in August 1992. However, just before final proofs were delivered the government published the Trade Union Reform and Employment Rights Bill which brings certain English provisions, particularly relating to maternity rights and consultations with trade unions, into line with EC directives and makes further more stringent demands upon the conduct of any pre-strike ballot. Where important changes have been made I have included reference to those changes in the appendix to the book, on the assumption that the Bill's provisions will not change between now and their enactment.

In most chapters of the book, save those relating to sex discrimination and maternity rights, I have used the masculine pronouns, but of course in all sections the contents of the book apply equally to both sexes.

I should like to thank in particular the series editor of this book, John Bowers, and Caroline Bates for their constructive comments and criticism, and Jo Hopgood and Nicolas Stevenson, without whose unfailing encouragement, support and help I might not have completed this book this year.

Julia Palca
November 1992

A The Contract of Employment, Employees' Rights and Obligations

Who is an employee?

A worker's relationship with his employer is primarily governed by the terms of the contract. The self-employed person has little else on which to rely; but an employee receives, in addition, numerous statutory rights and advantages. A description of these rights forms the majority of the subject-matter of this book. Who, then, are the people entitled to this cornucopia of benefits?

The law categorises workers under two main headings, those employed under 'contracts of service', who are employees, and those employed under 'contracts for services' who are freelance workers or independent contractors. The vast majority of employment law relates only to those employed under contracts of service. The main statutory provision which applies in both circumstances is the right not to be discriminated against on the grounds of race or sex. A further and important distinction is the resulting tax consequences. Those employed under 'contracts of service' are taxable under Schedule E and are subject to PAYE provisions. Self-employed people, on the other hand, are taxable under Schedule D and it is only in exceptional cases that tax is deducted at source. These include arrangements which sometimes operate in the printing industry, or which relate to foreign entertainers or sportsplayers who receive income in this country.

The contract

A contract of employment is created, just like other contracts, by an offer by one party which is accepted by the other, with both parties intending to create legal relations.

The commonly expressed view that 'an oral contract is not worth the paper it is written on' is incorrect. Elements of a contract of employment can be extracted from numerous different sources: contracts themselves, statements of particulars of the contract, express oral terms, implied terms, terms incorporated from other documents such as collective agreements or office manuals, and even obligations imposed by statute.

Employers have the obligation to give full-time employees, working at least 16 hours per week, a written statement of the particulars of certain terms of their employment. The statement must be given within 13 weeks of the commencement of employment. A prudent employer will, however, enter into a contract with the employee containing not only the topics which must be included in the written statement of particulars, but also the other aspects which will control the relationship between the parties.

The checklists in this chapter set out terms which have to be covered in any written statement of particulars, together with other terms which might be covered.

The contract may itself provide how it is to be terminated. In addition, the contract may be terminated by mutual agreement, by one party accepting another's breach of contract, by dismissal or even by frustration because circumstances that were not contemplated by the parties have intervened so that it has become impossible to perform the contract in the way originally envisaged. The non-renewal of a fixed-term contract will constitute a dismissal.

Varying the contract

In general, contracts can only be varied by consent. That consent can be express, or it can be implied by the employee continuing to work under the new terms, without protest, for a reasonable period of time. It is impossible to define precisely what this period would be, but it is likely to be a minimum of two months.

If an employer seeks to impose material changes in a contract of employment upon the employee, the employer will be in breach of the contract and the employee may accept this repudiatory breach, resign and claim constructive dismissal.

The safer course for an employer whose employees refuse to consent to variations in the terms of their employment is to give express notice to the employees terminating their contracts of employment, and at the same time offer them new contracts of employment on the varied terms. If the employer can show that there is a pressing business reason to change contractual terms such as pay, place of work, hours of work or even the abandonment of a particular union recognition agreement, he can argue that the variation is 'some other substantial reason' which would justify a fair dismissal. In order to do this, however, he must follow the requisite procedures, including consultation (see A.6).

An employee then has the options of accepting the offer of fresh employment, of rejecting it, or of accepting it only under protest. In the latter two cases the employee may claim that the termination of the original contract amounted to unfair dismissal or that the employer had no right to impose new terms and the original terms should continue to apply; it will then be for the employer to show that there was a pressing business reason which justified the change.

Consequences of breach of contract

If one party is in breach of the contract the other has the option of continuing with the contract but suing the first party for damages flowing from the breach, or terminating the contract and suing for damages flowing from the breach, and in either case of seeking an injunction restraining further breaches of contract. It will only be in the most exceptional circumstances that an injunction will be granted forcing an employer to continue to employ an individual, and public policy dictates that injunctions will not be granted forcing an individual to work for any particular employer.

Pay

It is an implied term of any contract of employment that the employer will remunerate the employee. Payment may be made in cash direct to the employee, by cheque, postal order or by direct transfer to the employee's bank or building society account. Only very limited deductions can be made from wages (which in the Wages Act 1986 are given a very broad definition to include commission, bonus, sick pay, maternity pay, and so on) without the employee's written consent.

A.1   WHO IS AN EMPLOYEE?

This issue is a question of fact and degree in each case. There is no clear rule, and various different tests have been used by the courts and tribunals. At present the courts look at the essence of the relationship between the parties and seek to decide whether or not an individual is an integrated part of the business for which he is working, or is in business on his own account.

A.1.1   Factors which indicate that an individual is an employee include:

A.1.1.1   PAYE and national insurance contributions are deducted at source from his income.

A.1.1.2   The individual receives holiday pay.

A.1.1.3   The individual is entitled to receive sick pay.

A.1.1.4   The individual is a member of an occupational pension scheme operated by the employer, or the employer contributes direct to a personal pension scheme for the employee.

A.1.1.5   The individual receives regular payments of salary/wages.

A.1.1.6   The individual is subject to an obligation not to work for rivals.

A.1.1.7   The individual is subject to the employer's disciplinary code.

A.1.2   General factors, too, come into play. Answers which indicate an independence on the part of the worker tend to show the worker is self-employed. Factors which go towards establishing the degree of control which an individual has over his own working life include:

A.1.2.1   The degree to which the individual is responsible for establishing the method of performing the tasks in hand.

A.1.2.2   The assumption by the individual of financial risk.

A.1.2.3   The permanence of the relationship.

A.1.2.4   Whether the individual has an opportunity to profit from sound management in the performance of his task.

A.1.2.5   The number of days worked by the individual for the employer.

A.1.2.6   The intention of the parties.

A.1.2.7   The method of computing the remuneration of the individual and the description of that remuneration, either as salary or fees.

A.1.2.8   Whether the individual charges VAT on the fees for his services.

A.1.3   Factors which would indicate that an individual is self-employed, under a contract for services, are that:

A.1.3.1   The individual owns his own tools.

A.1.3.2   The individual hires his own helpers.

A.1.3.3   The individual may substitute someone else to do a particular task commissioned by the employer.

A.1.3.4   The individual has responsibility for investment and management.

A.1.3.5   The individual is not obliged to work for the employer even if the employer so requests.

A.1.4   The rights and obligations of self-employed people will be determined entirely by the express and implied terms of the contract for services. Implicit in that contract is a term that the individual will carry out all contractual obligations, and will do so with reasonable skill and diligence. The employer, too, must fulfil his own contractual obligations and provide a safe work place. The only statutory employment obligations which apply to the self-employed are those which require people not to discriminate against the self-employed on the grounds of sex or race.

A.1.5 Employers are obliged to deduct income tax and national insurance contributions due from their employees at source under PAYE regulations. Employers in general have no such obligation to the self-employed, though the self-employed may charge VAT on their services. The Inland Revenue increasingly views claims to self-employed status with scepticism.

A.2 CONTENTS OF CONTRACT

A.2.1 Express terms

These may be written or oral. Examples of express terms are set out in A.4 and A.5.

A.2.2 Implied terms

These may be implied into the contract:

A.2.2.1 by the conduct of the parties (for example, if the parties have always behaved in a particular way which must have been anticipated by them when the contract was entered into, or by variation at a later stage); or

A.2.2.2 by custom and practice (which must be reasonable, certain and generally well-known); or

A.2.2.3 because terms are *necessary* to give efficacy to the agreement. One test is whether, if at the time the contract was entered into, an officious bystander were to ask whether a particular point was contained in the contract, the parties to the contract would have turned to him and have said 'of course'.

Implied terms and duties are considered in A.3.

A.2.3 Incorporated terms

Certain terms in other documents may be incorporated into the contract of employment, either expressly or by implication. Such documents include a collective agreement between the employer and a trade union of which the employee is a member; works rules; staff handbooks or office manuals. The following points apply:

A.2.3.1   Only those terms directly relating to the employee's contract, such as pay, benefits, hours, and duties are incorporated in the contract.

A.2.3.2   Provisions in collective agreements concerning the conduct of the relationship between employer and union, such as collective bargaining rights or disputes procedures, will generally not be incorporated into the individual's contract of employment.

A.2.3.3   A 'no strike clause' in a collective agreement can only be incorporated into an individual's contract of employment if:

A.2.3.3.1   the collective agreement is in writing;

A.2.3.3.2   the collective agreement contains an express statement that the clause is incorporated into individual contracts;

A.2.3.3.3   the collective agreement is reasonably accessible in the work place during work hours;

A.2.3.3.4   each trade union which is a party to the collective agreement is independent; and

A.2.3.3.5   the individual's contract of employment expressly or impliedly incorporates the collective agreement.

A.2.3.4   Provisions in works rules, staff handbooks and office manuals will only be incorporated into contracts of employment where they are always followed by custom and practice or where the parties must have intended them to have been included, such as sick pay schemes.

A.2.3.5   The following factors will indicate whether documents which are not expressly incorporated into any contract of employment are impliedly incorporated:

A.2.3.5.1   The nature of the document.

A.2.3.5.2   The methods used to bring the document to employees' attention.

A.2.3.5.3   Whether the document came into existence before or after the contract of employment began.

A.3   IMPLIED RIGHTS AND OBLIGATIONS

A.3.1   Implied terms and obligations on the part of the employee include:

A.3.1.1   The duty not to be negligent in performance of duties.

A.3.1.2   The duty to be reasonably competent to do the job.

A.3.1.3 The duty to co-operate with the employer in the performance of the job.

A.3.1.4 The duty to obey lawful and reasonable orders.

A.3.1.5 The duty of fidelity, for example:

A.3.1.5.1 The duty not to make secret profits during the course of employment, such as 'personal commissions', kickbacks or bribes. Such a profit could include a holiday for the employee. An employee offered such a 'perk' by a client or supplier of the employer should obtain the employer's consent before accepting.

A.3.1.5.2 The duty to disclose misdeeds on the part of others.

A.3.1.5.3 The duty not to take away the employer's property after termination of employment.

A.3.1.5.4 The duty to keep information confidential during the course of employment.

A.3.1.5.5 The duty to keep trade secrets confidential after the termination of employment.

A.3.1.5.6 The duty not to compete, nor to make preparations to compete, with the employer whilst still employed.

A.3.1.6 The duty to adapt to a new working environment or system, if reasonably introduced by the employer after proper training.

An employee who fails to honour these obligations will be in breach of his contract and may be disciplined by the employer. Any of the duties may be modified or extended by an express term dealing with the relevant topic.

A.3.2   Employee's rights implied by statute

A.3.2.1 The right to equal pay and to equal terms and conditions (see B.3).

A.3.2.2 The right to minimum notice periods (see A.8.1).

A.3.2.3 The right to 'guarantee pay' during non-working periods. This is a small daily sum, to be paid for a maximum of five days during any three-month non-working period.

A.3.2.4 The imposition of a maximum number of working hours per week in some cases — for example, certain maxima apply in industries such as mining, baking and lorry driving.

A.3.2.5   The right to receive statutory sick pay and statutory maternity pay (see C.4).

A.3.2.6   The right to inspect and, upon payment, to receive copies of any computerised personnel records, save the payroll, which the employer may keep. If any computerised personnel records are kept, the employer must register with the Data Protection Registrar.

A.3.3   In addition, the employee has the following *statutory rights*:

A.3.3.1   The right not to be discriminated against on grounds of sex, race or trade union membership (see B.4 and B.5).

A.3.3.2   The right not to be unfairly dismissed (for application see Chapter E).

A.3.3.3   The right to receive a redundancy payment (for application see Chapter F).

A.3.3.4   The right to an itemised pay statement.

A.3.3.5   The right of trade union officials to have paid or unpaid time off work in certain circumstances when taking part in trade union duties or activities, or when receiving training to enable them to do so.

A.3.3.6   The right of employees to unpaid time off work to perform certain public duties (for example as a Justice of the Peace, juror, school governor or member of a local authority or regional health authority) in certain circumstances.

A.3.4   *Duties and obligations imposed upon the employer* include:

A.3.4.1   To pay the employee.

A.3.4.2   To behave towards the employee with good faith. This can be sub-divided so that it obliges the employer:

A.3.4.2.1 Not without reasonable and proper cause to act in a manner likely to destroy the relationship of trust and confidence between employer and employee.

A.3.4.2.2   Not to treat employees arbitrarily, capriciously or inequitably regarding pay and other matters.

A.3.4.2.3   Not to undermine the authority of senior staff over their subordinates.

A.3.4.2.4   Not falsely to accuse employees of theft or other dishonest conduct.

A.3.4.3   Not to expect employees to work in intolerable conditions.

A.3.4.4   To treat staff with dignity. (Where breaches of this general provision constitute sexual harrassment, the employee may also complain of sex discrimination (see B.4.9).)

A.3.4.5   To take reasonable care for the safety of employees, for example in the selection of proper staff, the provision of adequate working materials, and the provision of a safe system of working.

A.3.4.6   Although there is no general duty upon employers to provide work for their employees, there is a duty to provide work for:

A.3.4.6.1   skilled or professional workers who need to work to maintain their skills (for example, scientists, doctors and other technicians),

A.3.4.6.2   employees who are paid partly by commission, such as members of a salesforce; and

A.3.4.6.3   trainees.

A.3.4.7   To provide training for employees required to operate new machinery or working practices.

A.3.4.8   If any reference is given (and an employer is not obliged to do so) it must be fair (see A.8.3).

If the employer is in serious breach of any of the obligations set out in A.3.4.1 to A.3.4.7, the employee may resign, claim constructive dismissal and both sue for damages for wrongful dismissal and claim compensation for unfair dismissal (see Chapter E). If there is a breach of A.3.4.8, the employee may bring proceedings for damages for any loss suffered and for libel, but to succeed in a libel action the employee will have to show that the employer was actuated by malice in giving an unfair reference. In the absence of malice, the employer should be able successfully to defend any libel action on the ground of qualified privilege.

A.4   **WRITTEN STATEMENT OF TERMS**

A.4.1   An employer must give each employee, within 13 weeks of the commencement of employment, a written statement containing certain particulars of the terms of employment. (See Appendix.)

A.4.2   If there is any variation in the particulars of employment, the employer must give the employee a complete amended statement within one month, unless the variation relates only to the name of the employer or identity of employer (where the Transfer of Undertakings Regulations apply, see Chapter G), in which case only a notice informing employees of the change of name or identity is necessary.

A.4.3   **Methods of giving particulars**

A.4.3.1   By giving the employee a contract of employment incorporating the relevant particulars.

A.4.3.2   By giving the employee a copy of a written statement setting out the particulars.

A.4.3.3   By providing access to a document containing the provisions of employment, for example a document on the staff notice board.

A.4.3.4   By referring, in a contract or statement of particulars, to another document to which the employee can gain access, which sets out relevant details.

A.4.4   **Obligatory contents of particulars**

                The particulars must set out contractual provisions relating to the following matters (and if there are no relevant provisions, the statement must say so):

A.4.4.1   Identity of employer.

A.4.4.2   Identity of employee.

A.4.4.3   The date when employment began.

A.4.4.4   Whether any previous service counts as continuous with the present contract.

A.4.4.5   Job title.

A.4.4.6   Scale or rate of remuneration, or the method of calculating remuneration.

A.4.4.7   The intervals at which remuneration is paid (for example, weekly or monthly).

A.4.4.8   Normal hours of work.

A.4.4.9   Entitlement to public and other holidays and holiday pay.

A.4.4.10   Provision for sickness and injury, including sick pay.

A.4.4.11   Pension rights, and whether a contracting-out certificate has been given under the Social Security Pensions Act 1975.

A.4.4.12   Notice period, or if the contract is a fixed-term contract, the date that term expires.

A.4.4.13   Grievance procedures.

A.4.4.14   (When more than 20 people are employed on the date the employee's employment began) disciplinary procedures. (See Appendix.)

A.4.5   The contents of a written statement of particulars are prima facie, but not conclusive, evidence of the terms of the contract. If no particulars are given, or if the particulars which are given are wrong, an industrial tribunal may determine what the particulars should have contained, or what amendments should be made. No sanction, however, may be imposed upon an employer who fails to give the particulars.

A.5   OTHER EXPRESS CONTRACTUAL PROVISIONS

A.5.1   Other topics which may be of relevance to employment are not incorporated by implication into the contract of employment. If the parties therefore wish the contract to refer to these matters, they must do so expressly. Such topics include:

A.5.1.1   Whether the employee is obliged to work overtime and if so to what extent.

A.5.1.2   Whether the employee is able to take up other employment outside working hours.

A.5.1.3   Whether the employee should have more onerous confidentiality obligations than are implied by law (see A.3.1.5.4 and A.3.1.5.5).

A.5.1.4   Whether the employee consents to certain deductions being made from wages. If no such consent is given, in general no deductions can be made. The employer might want the ability to make deductions if any fine is imposed pursuant to a disciplinary procedure, or if there are till or stock shortages (see A.9).

A.5.1.5   Whether the employer is entitled to institute layoff or short-time working on no pay or on reduced pay. The employer has no right to impose layoff or short-time working without pay unless there is an express contractual provision to that effect or this is an established custom and practice.

A.5.1.6   A 'garden leave' clause, enabling an employer to suspend an employee from performing work (such a clause will only be enforced by the courts by way of injunction if there is a significant risk to the employer of breach of confidential information, and so long as the employee continues to receive full pay and benefits). This clause may assist an employer whose employee has given notice, and who thinks the employee has confidential information regarding, for example, current contracts with customers, pricing policy or a strong customer connection, which will become less valuable to the employee's future employer after a particular time period has expired.

A.5.1.7   What duties the employee may be required to perform: it is in the employer's interest for the contract to be flexible so that the employer can, under the contract, require the employee to perform a variety of tasks (for example, 'the employee shall perform such duties as may from time to time be given to the employee by X').

A.5.1.8   A contractual term, for employees on fixed-term contracts of two years or more, excluding the employee's right to compensation for unfair dismissal or redundancy if the contract expires at the end of the term. Such an expiry would otherwise count as a dismissal.

A.5.1.9   Express terms regarding the ownership of all rights in the product of the employee's work, whether written, artistic or scientific. In the absence of contractual assignments of copyright or patent rights, the statutory position is as follows:

A.5.1.9.1   The employer is the first owner of the copyright in any work created by the employee in the normal course of work for the employer.

A.5.1.9.2   A patent in any invention made by the employee in the normal course of duty will belong to the employer. The employee is always entitled to such a fair share of profits from any invention as is reasonable in all the circumstances.

Note that these provisions do *not* apply to the self-employed, who are generally first owners of intellectual property rights in their own creations.

A.⁵.2   For more senior employees or sales staff, employers should also consider the imposition of *restrictive covenants*. These must not be in restraint of trade, nor must they be penal. They must do no more than protect the employer's business. They must be reasonable. Restrictive covenants normally relate to the following aspects of an ex-employee's activities:

A.5.2.1   The area in which the employee cannot compete with the employer for a particular period after termination.

A.5.2.2   The sections of the employer's business with which the employee cannot compete for a particular period after termination (such a covenant will only be valid in rare circumstances).

A.5.2.3   Non-solicitation of the employer's customers with whom the employee has had an established connection or has had contact, for a particular period after termination.

A.5.2.4   Not dealing, either directly or indirectly, with any of the employer's customers with whom the employee has an established connection for a particular period after termination. This is a wider covenant than that in A.5.2.3, and includes circumstances where customers have sought out the former employee of their own accord. The period of the restriction should therefore never be longer than the period of a non-solicitation covenant.

A.5.2.5   Not enticing away the employer's other employees for a particular period after termination.

A.5.2.6   Not directly or indirectly employing the employer's other employees for a particular period after termination.

A.5.3   Employers may wish to be able summarily to terminate employees' contracts of employment and pay them a particular sum, for example the remuneration which they would have received for the balance of the contract period. Any sums payable pursuant to this section will be taxed under normal Schedule E provisions. Should there not be such a clause, employees could argue that the payment of monies in lieu of notice is a breach of contract in not allowing them to work out the notice. The main reason for incorporating such a provision is to preserve restrictive covenants in a contract: if the employer terminates the contract without giving due notice, a breach of the contract will have been committed as a result of which the employer will no longer be able to enforce any of the restrictive covenants contained in the contract.

A.6   VARYING CONTRACT TERMS

A.6.1   The employer should check to see whether the terms of the present contract are sufficiently flexible to allow him lawfully to make the required changes.

A.6.2   The employer should check that there is no legal impediment which would make the variation difficult to sustain. For example, the Shops Act 1950 may prevent employers in certain retail sectors from requiring employees to work on Sundays.

A.6.3   If A.6.1 and/or A.6.2 do not apply, the employer should seek the consent of the employees to any variation. Consent may be express, or tacit. Tacit consent would probably be inferred if the employee continued to work, adopting the changes, without protest for a reasonable period. The length of the period would depend upon the circumstances, but should be at least two months.

A.6.4   Employers should consider 'buying out' unwanted terms by paying employees to agree to contractual variations.

A.6.5   If agreement cannot be reached on any variation, and provided the employer has a pressing business need to implement a variation, the employer should proceed as follows:

A.6.5.1   Consult with the employees, explaining the pressing business need which makes the variation necessary, and what terms are proposed.

A.6.5.2   Formulate reasonable new contract terms within the context of the employer's pressing business requirements; in doing so, the interests of the employees cannot be ignored, so the employer should not seek to impose totally draconian new terms.

A.6.5.3   Terminate the old contracts by giving proper notice, and in this regard the employer should comply with contractual provisions relating to consultation or warnings of impending terminations and the general obligation to behave reasonably before dismissal.

A.6.5.4   Introduce new contracts of employment.

A.6.6 An employee who does not wish to accept any variations may:

A.6.6.1 If *variations are wrongfully imposed* by the employer:

A.6.6.1.1 work under protest and bring proceedings in the High Court or county court against the employer for damages for breach of contract or for sums due under the contract; or

A.6.6.1.2 resign, claim constructive dismissal, and sue for damages for wrongful and, if appropriate, unfair dismissal (see Chapter E).

A.6.6.1.3 If variation consists of deduction from wages bring a Wages Act claim in the industrial tribunal.

A.6.6.2 If the *employer has acted correctly* in accordance with the provisions of A.6.5:

A.6.6.2.1 accept the new job; or

A.6.6.2.2 accept the new job under protest, argue that the changes imposed cannot be justified by any pressing business reason of the employer, and claim compensation for having been unfairly dismissed by the termination of the original contract and the restoration of the original contract terms; or

A.6.6.2.3 refuse to accept the new job, argue that the proposed new terms could not be justified by a pressing business need, and claim unfair dismissal.

A.6.7 An employer has a duty to notify individual employees of any changes to the contract of employment, such as changes negotiated by the employer with the employee's trade union.

A.6.8 On a transfer of undertaking there must be an economic, technical or organisational reason justifying the change in terms. In general, if the new employer's existing staff are employed on worse contractual provisions than those acquired pursuant to a transfer of undertaking, the employer should not worsen the transferred employees' contractual terms: to do so will normally automatically be unfair. It is normally very difficult to harmonise the terms and conditions of employment following the acquisition of an undertaking (see G.4.4 and G.4.5).

A.7 BREACH OF CONTRACT

A.7.1 If the *employee* breaches a contract the employer may:

A.7.1.1   If the breach is sufficiently material, dismiss the employee.

A.7.1.2   Sue the employee in the High Court or county court for damages for breach of contract. Given that most employees have limited financial resources to pay damages, this tactic is normally only employed as a counterclaim to any claim for wrongful dismissal brought by the employee (see E.2).

A.7.1.3   Refuse to pay the employee the whole of the wages due for any period during which the employee takes industrial action and does not perform part or all of his duties.

A.7.1.4   Obtain an injunction restraining future breaches of the contract if the employer can show that such breaches are likely to recur, that damages are an inadequate remedy, that he will suffer loss as a result of the breaches, and that the balance of convenience is in favour of granting the injunction.

A.7.2   If the *employer* is in breach of contract the employee may:

A.7.2.1   Protest at the breaches but continue to work and bring proceedings against the employer in the High Court or county court for sums due under the contract or for damages for breach of contract.

A.7.2.2   If sufficiently serious, resign, claim constructive dismissal, and damages and compensation for wrongful and/or unfair dismissal.

A.7.2.3   In exceptional circumstances, obtain an injunction restraining breaches of contract by the employer. Such injunctions are only granted very rarely (for example, where the employer fails properly to follow disciplinary procedures) and will not be granted if a court is convinced that the relationship of trust and confidence between employer and employee has irretrievably broken down.

A.8   TERMINATION OF CONTRACT

A.8.1   Notice periods

A.8.1.1   If no notice period is expressed in the contract of employment, the court will imply a reasonable notice period. For manual or semi-skilled workers, that notice period is likely to be between one week and one month; for middle-ranking employees, the notice period will be between one and three months; and for senior employees, the notice period will be between three months and, say, one year.

A.8.1.2   In addition, there are statutory minimum notice periods which override lesser contractual provisions:

A.8.1.2.1   Once an employee has been employed for one month, he is obliged to give at least one week's notice of termination of his employment.

A.8.1.2.2   Once an employee has been employed for one month, he is entitled to receive a minimum notice period of one week during the first two years of his employment, and thereafter is entitled to one week's notice for each completed year of employment up to a maximum of 12 weeks.

A.8.1.3   *Example* An employee with a contractual notice period of one month on either side has been employed for 7½ years. The employee is entitled to 7 weeks' notice.

A.8.1.4   An employee is obliged not to leave his employment before the expiry of his notice period, unless the employer agrees. An employee who resigns without giving notice:

A.8.1.4.1   Cannot be forced to return to work.

A.8.1.4.2   May be restrained by an injunction obtained by the employer from joining a rival, provided the employer will actually suffer damage if the employee leaves early, for example if the employee proposes to join a competing business.

     The employer must undertake to provide the employee with full contractual remuneration and benefits for the entire notice period, and must satisfy the court that all the other preconditions for the grant of interlocutory injunctions exist (see D.6.1.4 to D.6.1.7). An injunction will not be granted if the employee is subject to a long notice period and can satisfy the court that relevant skills he possesses will atrophy if the employee cannot exercise them during the notice period.

A.8.1.5   If an employer terminates an employee's contract of employment without giving due notice, the employee may bring an action against the employer for wrongful dismissal to recover the sums he would have received during the balance of the notice period. The employee nevertheless has an obligation to mitigate his loss. (For the position on wrongful dismissal see E.2.)

A.8.2   Methods of termination of the contract

A.8.2.1   By consent of both parties (although if the employer forces the employee to consent, this would be construed as a dismissal).

A.8.2.2   By either party giving the requisite notice to the other. Even if the employer gives the employee proper notice, there may still be grounds for the employee to claim compensation for unfair dismissal or redundancy.

A.8.2.3   By expiry of a fixed-term contract. Unless the fixed-term contract specifically excludes the employee's right to compensation for unfair dismissal or to a redundancy payment upon the expiry of the contract, such expiry can nevertheless be an unfair dismissal or redundancy. If the contract continues after its expiry, it will continue on the same terms as before, and will be terminable on reasonable notice.

A.8.2.4   By frustration — if it becomes impossible for the parties to perform the contract at all or in substantially the same way as was envisaged when the contract was entered into. Examples include the absence of the employee because of long-term ill health or imprisonment, or because a material work permit expires or cannot be transferred from a previous employer.

A.8.2.5   By dismissal by the employer. This may be fair or unfair.

A.8.2.6   By the employee resigning following a repudiatory breach of contract by the employer and claiming constructive dismissal.

A.8.2.7   Following a pregnancy, if an employee who has the right to return does not exercise that right or if the employer refuses to allow the employee to return. Such a refusal is likely to amount to an unfair dismissal.

A.8.2.8   By operation of law, for example if a statute is passed rendering further performance impossible.

A.8.3   References

An employer is not obliged to give any employee a reference. References are normally given on occasions of qualified privilege. If the employer does so, the reference must be fair and accurate and made without malice. If it is not:

A.8.3.1   a subsequent employer may sue the original employer for negligent/fraudulent mis-statement, if the reference is inaccurate and he can show that the employer must have known this, or did not take care to ensure that it was accurate;

A.8.3.2   the employee may sue the employer for defamation, if he can show the employer was acting maliciously, i.e., that he knew the reference was false, or was reckless as to whether or not it was true or false.

A.9 PAY

A.9.1 During the course of employment the employer can only make the following deductions from the employee's wages.

A.9.1.1 Deductions required by statute such as PAYE and national insurance contributions.

A.9.1.2 Any deduction to which the employee has consented in writing.

A.9.1.3 Any payment to a third party to which the employee has consented in writing.

A.9.1.4 Any deductions made within a reasonable time for reimbursement of previous overpayments of wages or expenses.

A.9.1.5 Any deductions made on account of an employee's participation in industrial action (including not only pay but also any damages suffered by the employer as a result of the industrial action).

A.9.1.6 Any payments the employer is required by statute to make to a public authority following an appropriate order (for example, paying community charge payments).

A.9.1.7 Any sums the employer is required to pay pursuant to an attachment of earnings order made by the court.

The word 'wages' is very widely defined and includes fees, bonuses, commissions and holiday pay but not pay in lieu of notice.

A.9.2 Special provisions apply in the retail industry, where, even if the employee has consented in writing to deductions being made, deductions in any period to compensate for stock deficiencies or cash shortages (or any payments the employee is required to make as a result of deficiencies or shortages) cannot exceed 10 per cent of the employee's gross wages for the relevant period.

A.9.3 If the employer wrongfully makes deduction from pay or makes no payment whatsoever, the employee may complain to an industrial tribunal within three months of the relevant deduction, or of the last deduction in the series, seeking an order for payment of the sums due. The employee may also, if he so wishes, bring proceedings in a county court or High Court for damages for breach of contract but cannot recover more than once in respect of any particular deduction.

A.9.4   The employer must give the employee an itemised pay statement showing gross pay; all deductions such as those for tax, national insurance contributions, pension payments or any trade union subscription; and the net amount receivable.

B   Equal Pay and Discrimination

Employers who adopt discriminatory practices do so at their peril. The Equal Pay Act 1970 (EqPA), the Sex Discrimination Act 1975 (SDA), the Race Relations Act 1976 as amended (RRA), the Employment Protection (Consolidation) Act 1978 (EPCA) and, to a limited extent, the Employment Acts 1989 and 1990 between them provide that employers cannot discriminate between people of different sexes and races in their selection procedures, contractual terms and treatment of employees, and also cannot discriminate against those who are or are not trade union members in the appointment of and treatment of their employees. In this chapter, potential complainants are described as female, though the points apply equally to males.

Equal pay

If an employee shows she does substantially similar work to a named member of the opposite sex, or performs work which has been rated as equivalent work under a job evaluation scheme, or is of equal or greater value than work carried out by a named member of the opposite sex, and any element of the employee's contractual terms is worse than that of the chosen comparator, the EqPA operates to bring the worse contractual term up to the same level as the better one. Each element that makes up a contract of employment is looked at individually, and employers cannot rely upon a general balancing out of benefits under the contract as a whole. Once an employee has shown that her job is substantially the same as or of equal value to the job of a member of the opposite sex, the employer's only excuse for any different contractual terms can be that some other material factor exists, such as length of service or degree of skill, which justifies the differential in pay or benefits. The Act applies not only to wages but to all contractual terms such as bonus, holiday entitlement, car policies and sickness benefits. Employees who are successful are entitled in future to remuneration and benefits on the higher level enjoyed by their comparator, and to have the difference refunded for the period starting two years before the court or tribunal application was made.

The EqPA applies Article 119 of the Treaty of Rome and various EC directives on equal treatment. Article 119 also has direct force in Great Britain. For example, an employee can compare her terms and conditions under Article 119 with those of an employee of the opposite sex who was not employed at any time during the period of the complainant's employment. Its ambit is wider than the EqPA, so that an employee with no remedy under the EqPA, but with a potential remedy under Article 119, can still bring proceedings in an industrial tribunal in the normal way.

Sex Discrimination Act

The EqPA and the SDA compliment each other. While the EqPA deals with contractual terms, the SDA deals with all other aspects of employment, from recruitment, through career structure to dismissal. The SDA applies not only to direct acts of discrimination, where an employee can show that a member of the opposite sex has been treated more favourably on any particular matter, but also to indirect discrimination. This applies when employers have a rule, which applies to both sexes, but which, when examined, appears strongly to disadvantage the members of one sex. Obvious examples are rules which require people to be of a particular height, or which disadvantage part-time workers (given that women form a substantial majority of the part-time workforce). Once employees can show that they are being treated less favourably than a named person, or even that they are being treated less favourably than a hypothetical member of the opposite sex, the employer's only defences are that the complainants would have been treated exactly the same had they been of the opposite sex, or that sex was a genuine occupational qualification for the job.

Race Relations Act 1976

Employers must not discriminate on the grounds of colour, race, nationality or ethnic or national origins against any person of either sex. This applies not only to recruitment policies, treatment during employment and career structures, and dismissal, but also to contractual terms. The provisions relating to race discrimination are substantially the same as those relating to sex discrimination, and are therefore not dealt with separately in this book.

Trade union discrimination

Since 1971 it has been unlawful to discriminate against individuals if the purpose is to prevent or deter them from being a trade union member, or from taking part in the activities of a trade union. Now, too, it is unlawful to use recruitment procedures to discriminate against people who are or who are not trade union members.

The disabled

There is no law which prevents employers from discriminating against the disabled on that ground alone (although obviously the disabled cannot be discriminated against on grounds of sex, race or trade union membership). It is an offence under the Disabled Persons (Employment) Acts 1944 and 1958 for employers with 20 or more employees to have a quota of less than 3 per cent of their workforce who are registered disabled. It is also an offence to dismiss someone who is a registered disabled person if to do so would put the employer below his required quota. Since employers may seek exemptions from the scheme (and a substantial number have) and the law is not enforceable directly by the individual, these provisions are in fact largely ignored.

B.1 WHICH ACT DOES A CLAIM FALL UNDER?

B.1.1 Equal Pay Act 1970

This applies to employees, apprentices and self-employed people under a contract personally to perform services for someone other than pursuant to a contractor-client relationship, and will cover the following:

B.1.1.1 Pay.

B.1.1.2 Bonuses.

B.1.1.3 Concessions and benefits in kind.

B.1.1.4 Terms in collective agreements.

B.1.1.5 General contractual provisions such as those regarding holidays, sickness benefits and hours.

Indirect discrimination (as to which see B.2.2.3 and B.2.2.4) will not found a complaint under EqPA. The following, too, are not covered by the Act:

— Terms effected in compliance with the law regarding women's employment.

— Terms relating to pregnancy and childbirth.

— Terms regarding death or retirement, save that retirement ages must be the same and access to occupational pension schemes must be equal.

— Any differential imposed on grounds of marital status alone.

B.1.2   **Article 119, Treaty of Rome**

This gives employees complaining of discrimination in the terms and conditions of their contracts of employment additional rights in the following areas:

B.1.2.1   In circumstances where a comparator is not employed contemporaneously with the applicant.

B.1.2.2   Claims relating to payments and benefits under occupational pension schemes, whether contributory or non-contributory.

B.1.2.3   Contractual and ex-gratia payments made following a compulsory redundancy.

B.1.2.4   Indirect discrimination regarding contractual terms (for examples see B.2.2.3 and B.2.2.4).

B.1.3   **Sex Discrimination Act 1975 and Race Relations Act 1976**

These apply to all applicants, employees, temporary workers supplied by employment agencies and self-employed people under a contract personally to perform services for someone other than pursuant to a contractor-client relationship in the following areas:

B.1.3.1   Arrangements for recruitment (whether or not anyone is in fact recruited).

B.1.3.2   Recruitment advertisements.

B.1.3.3   Non-contractual benefits.

B.1.3.4   Occupational pension schemes.

B.1.3.5   Opportunities for promotion and transfer.

B.1.3.6   Training opportunities (save in a case where positive training of particular groups is allowed – see B.4.5.2).

B.1.3.7   Sexual harrassment or sustained racial abuse.

B.1.3.8   Grounds for dismissal.

B.1.3.9   Contractual benefits (RRA only).

B.1.3.10   SDA also prevents people from discriminating on the ground of marital status.

B.1.4 **Employment Protection (Consolidation) Act 1978, as amended**

B.1.4.1 Claims that a person has been subject to discriminatory treatment during the course of employment as a result of her membership of a trade union or lack of it.

B.1.4.2 Claims that a person has been dismissed as a result of her participation in the affairs of a recognised trade union at an appropriate time.

B.1.5 **Employment Act 1990**

Claims that a person has been refused offers of employment on the ground of her trade union membership or lack of it.

B.2 **TESTS**

B.2.1 **Equal pay**

If people are employed upon like work, work of equal value, or work rated as equivalent under a job evaluation scheme, and are of different sexes, they should receive similar terms and conditions of employment unless there is a genuine material difference between the cases which justifies the differential. The test only applies to direct discrimination, where someone can compare herself with a person employed at the same establishment with differing terms, and where that person is of the opposite sex. It does not allow two people of the same sex to compare their salaries.

B.2.2 **Sex and race discrimination: direct and indirect**

B.2.2.1 The basic test is whether the individual would have received the same treatment from the employer or potential employer but for his or her own sex or race. Motive for the different treatment is irrelevant.

B.2.2.2 Discrimination may be direct, or indirect. Direct discrimination occurs when a person is receiving less favourable treatment on account of his/her sex, marital status or race.

B.2.2.3 *Indirect discrimination*

The Sex and Race Discrimination Acts also apply in connection with indirect discrimination, where a requirement or condition is made, apparently applying to everyone, but which subtly discriminates against a class of people, the majority of whom are of one sex or race. To test whether a requirement or condition amounts to indirect discrimination:

B.2.2.3.1   Identify the criteria for selection.

B.2.2.3.2   Identify the relevant pool of potential candidates.

B.2.2.3.3   Divide the pool into those who satisfy the criteria and those who do not.

B.2.2.3.4   Predict statistically what proportion of each sex or race should consist of women, by comparison with the total number employed in the appropriate pool — for example, all those people in England in a similar situation, or all those performing similar tasks.

B.2.2.3.5   Compare the actual findings with the statistically produced findings. If members of one sex are under-represented in comparison with the statistics, this is potentially discriminatory.

B.2.2.4   Examples of indirect discrimination:

B.2.2.4.1   Requirement that people should be of a certain height.

B.2.2.4.2   Treatment that disadvantages part-time workers, many of whom tend to be women.

B.2.2.4.3   Treatment that disadvantages workers with young children (which may discriminate on the grounds of marital status).

B.2.2.4.4   Special treatment of workers from a particular area with a predominantly ethnic population.

B.2.2.4.5   Imposition of language tests which would exclude large numbers from ethnic minority groups.

B.2.2.4.6   Requirement that candidates should have a long period of previously uninterrupted working — which tends to exclude women who have taken time off work to look after children.

B.2.2.4.7   Requirement that applicants should be aged 25 to 35 (which excludes many women with young children).

B.2.2.5   The defences to an allegation of indirect discrimination are either that the conditions which have been imposed are justifiable on reasonable, non-sexual or racial grounds, for example because of economic or administrative reasons, safety, hygiene or management experience; or that the conditions have caused no detriment to the applicant.

B.3   **EQUAL PAY ACT — CONTRACTS OF EMPLOYMENT**

B.3.1   **What the employee must show**

If an employee believes that her terms and conditions of employment are worse than those of a man, she should:

B.3.1.1   Establish that the Act applies. It applies to:

B.3.1.1.1   Any employee.

B.3.1.1.2   Any apprentice.

B.3.1.1.3   Any self-employed person who is personally to perform services.

It does not apply to those based outside Great Britain.

B.3.1.2   Establish what is the difference in terms and conditions of employment, for example is there a difference in:

B.3.1.2.1   Pay.

B.3.1.2.2   Hours of work.

B.3.1.2.3   Method of allocation of bonuses or size of bonuses.

B.3.1.2.4   Incentive payments.

B.3.1.2.5   Concessions and benefits in kind such as advantageous loans, mortgage repayment allowances, participation in insurance schemes or share option schemes.

B.3.1.2.6   Provisions in collective agreements incorporated into the contracts of employment.

B.3.1.2.7   Terms relating to holidays, sickness benefits and other contractual provisions.

B.3.1.3   Choose a comparator. That comparator must be a genuine individual, and not a hypothetical case. Under the EqPA, the comparator must have been employed at the same time as the complainant, but under European law the complainant may, if she wishes, compare herself with her predecessor or her replacement.

B.3.1.3.1   The comparator must work at the same establishment. This is a question of fact, depending upon the following factors:

— The degree of exclusive occupation of the premises.

— The degree of permanence of the arrangements.

— The organisation of workers — whether they are organised as part of one group, or in separate and distinct entities.

— How the administration is organised — if there is central administration and the head office runs several sites, such as building sites, those sites are likely to be part of the same establishment. If each site is separately run, such as branches of a chain of shops, each site is likely to be a separate establishment.

B.3.1.3.2   If the comparator is not working at the same establishment, is she working at an establishment where similar terms and conditions apply for the relevant class of employee? This must be the case, for example, where a collective agreement applies to both establishments. If similar terms and conditions apply, the establishments may be owned by associated companies and not only by the employer.

B.3.1.4   Establish whether the comparator is engaged upon like work. This is a question of fact, bearing in mind the following questions:

B.3.1.4.1   Do the two have the same job title?

B.3.1.4.2   Do the two carry out the same basic process? This may be broadly defined, and the tribunal will look to see whether the jobs are substantially similar, and not whether they are identical (see B.3.1.4.3). For example, a chef in a directors' dining room may do similar work to a cook in the works canteen.

B.3.1.4.3   If there are differences, what are their nature and extent, and how frequently do they operate? If they operate infrequently (for example, if occasionally a man is asked to undertake heavy work) or are minor (for example, where canteen ladies sometimes waited at tables whereas their male comparator did not) work will still be regarded as like.

B.3.1.5   Establish whether the employer has carried out a job evaluation scheme, and if so whether the two jobs rated by that scheme are equivalent. If they are, yet terms and conditions of employment between people of opposite sexes are different, the employee will succeed. If they are not rated as equivalent, an employee will only succeed in a claim for equal pay if she can show that discriminatory criteria were used in setting up the job evaluation scheme, or that the scheme has not been put into effect and complied with.

B.3.1.6   Ascertain whether the comparator is engaged on work of equal value. This is a nebulous test. If the applicant believes that her work is of equal value to that carried out by a man — and the work of a cook has been held by the courts to be of equal value to that of a painter, joiner and thermal installation engineer — she should apply to an industrial tribunal for a job study to be carried out by an independent expert. To make the application, she must show that there may be grounds for deciding that her work is of equal value to a male comparator. If an industrial tribunal decides that there is a case to answer, it must invite the parties to seek to conciliate, and, if that fails, a report by an independent expert is commissioned. Either party can seek to disallow the report if procedural requirements have not been complied with, if the evidence could never justify the conclusion, or if it is unsatisfactory for some other material reason. If the report is rejected, another will be commissioned. This route is lengthy and cumbersome.

B.3.1.7   Attempt to show that a man who has worked in the same establishment as her, or one with similar terms and conditions, and who performs like work, work rated as equivalent or work of equal value, has advantageous terms and conditions of employment. If she establishes this, prima facie, she has proved discrimination.

B.3.2   The employer's response

The employer can only successfully defend a claim for equal pay if he can show either that the employee's allegations are incorrect, for example that the employee and the comparator have never worked in the same establishment or that the work is not similar, or that there is a genuine material factor other than sex which justifies the differential.

B.3.2.1   *Work not 'like'*

Where the employee has claimed that she is engaged in 'like' work to her comparator, the employer should look at the make-up of the job and examine whether there are important differences between the two. If the employer can show that the work is not like, the employee's claim fails. Differences may include:

B.3.2.1.1   One employee habitually undertakes more night work.

B.3.2.1.2   One employee handles more substantial sums of money or more valuable goods.

B.3.2.1.3   One employee habitually performs heavier work.

B.3.2.1.4   One employee has the obligation frequently to work overtime.

B.3.2.1.5   One employee's work is more dangerous.

B.3.2.1.6   One employee has more responsibility than the other.

B.3.2.2   *Job evaluation scheme*

If a job evaluation scheme has been carried out which does not place the positions of the applicant and her comparator on the same grade, the applicant will generally not succeed in her claim. The scheme must not have been based on discriminatory factors, must have been put into effect and must have been complied with. There are four main methods of conducting job evaluation schemes, which are normally undertaken by experts. These are:

B.3.2.2.1   Job ranking — each job is considered as a whole and then ranked in comparison with other jobs.

B.3.2.2.2   Paired comparisons — as above but each job is considered in relation to one other, then graded.

B.3.2.2.3   Job classification — jobs are valued according to a benchmark grade.

B.3.2.2.4   Points assessment — jobs are broken down into component parts such as skill, hours and qualifications.

B.3.2.3   *Material difference*

Even if the two individuals are engaged on like work, or if their work is rated as equivalent under a job evaluation scheme, if the employer can show that there is a genuine material difference other than sex between the two cases which causes the *whole* of the difference, the employee's claim will fail. If the difference only explains part of the variation, then the employee's claim will succeed. Material differences include:

B.3.2.3.1   Qualifications.

B.3.2.3.2   Level of experience.

B.3.2.3.3   Level of service.

B.3.2.3.4   Degree of skills acquired.

B.3.2.3.5   Responsibilities undertaken.

B.3.2.3.6   Regional pay variations.

B.3.2.3.7   Different economic circumstances affecting the business itself where the comparator was working at a different time from the complainant.

B.3.2.3.8   That the individuals are in differing levels in the grading structure.

B.3.2.3.9   That market forces have dictated that a later applicant is paid more (or less) than someone who is already established in the job.

B.3.2.3.10   Part-time working — but this can only be a justification if the differential between part-time and full-time rates is justifible on economic grounds, for example if short-time working costs more because machinery is lying idle for longer, and provided too that part-time workers of both sexes are paid the same.

B.3.2.3.11   The comparator is a 'red circled' worker (i.e. where the comparator has been demoted but her pay has not been reduced) although the differential in pay should be phased out over time, and there should be no outsiders within the 'red circle'.

B.3.2.3.12   Unintentional indirect discrimination. However, any rule which operates disproportionately, with some actual barrier, condition or requirement between two positions, must be objectively justified. If members of a predominently female group can transfer to a predominantly male group, and hence receive greater benefits, there will probably be no discrimination. If transfer is difficult or impossible, there may be discrimination.

B.3.2.4   *Work not of equal value*

B.3.2.4.1   See B.3.1.6.

B.3.2.4.2   If an independent report has concluded that the complainant's work is of equal value to a comparator, this claim can be defeated on the basis that there is a genuine material factor causing the difference. 'Factor' can encompass any issue, and not merely a material difference between the woman's case and the man's, and factors would include all those examples cited in 3.2.3, and all market forces claims, even where a lone individual demands, and receives, a higher wage.

B.3.3   **Bringing the claim**

B.3.3.1   The complainant may bring a claim in the industrial tribunal or the county court, but must do so during employment or within six months of leaving employment. The claim under EqPA may relate back for two years. Applications under Article 119 may have no time limit.

B.3.3.2   The employee may seek help from the Equal Opportunities Commission in bringing her claim, who may agree to fund all or part of the cost of the application.

B.3.3.3   There is no maximum award in any equal pay claim. The award is the difference between the value of the applicant's and the comparator's pay and conditions during the period from up to two years before the date the application was made to the date of the hearing. For the future, the contract is varied so that thereafter the pay must be equal. Claims under Article 119 may have no time limit.

B.4   **CLAIMS RELATING TO OTHER ASPECTS OF EMPLOYMENT**

The SDA and RRA seek to ensure that all people are treated equally at all stages of employment regardless of sex, marital status or race (it is lawful to discriminate against single persons). If people are not treated equally, prima facie they have a valid discrimination complaint. The following factors apply specifically:

B.4.1   **Arrangements for recruitment**

B.4.1.1   Recruitment advertisements should not include words with any sexual connotation unless there is a genuine occupational qualification which requires someone of a particular sex or race for the job (see B.5.2, B.5.3 and B.5.4). If there is a genuine occupational qualification, the employer should inform the publisher of the advertisement, or any employment agency which he uses, of that fact, since they are also subject to penalties if a discriminatory advertisement is published. The employer, too, may be fined if incorrect information is given to an employment agency. Examples of potentially discriminatory advertisements include:

B.4.1.1.1   those which have pictures of successful applicants, all or most of whom are of one sex or race;

B.4.1.1.2   those which use terms with a male connotation, such as post*men*. Instead of using such terms, one should use neutral terms (for example, fire fighter), or terms applying to both sexes (for example, postman/postwoman) or include a statement that 'men and women can apply', or that the employer is an equal opportunities employer;

B.4.1.1.3   those which state that the successful candidate must be able to meet a condition or qualification which would not usually be required for the job, but which would apply unequally to the sexes or races, or to married people. For example, a statement that the successful candidate would have to work anti-social hours if this happens rarely, might be discriminatory for it could discriminate against women and/or married persons.

B.4.1.2   Job descriptions should relate to the vacancy rather than the sex or race of the individual and should not contain discriminatory wording.

B.4.1.3   Application forms or selection tests, where used, should not contain any discriminatory questions but should focus upon the previous relevant experience of the individual.

B.4.2   **Employment agencies**

Careers offices and employment agencies must not discriminate when providing:

B.4.2.1   Careers advice.

B.4.2.2   Information about jobs.

B.4.2.3   Job interviews.

B.4.2.4   Placements in jobs.

B.4.2.5   Any other employment service.

B.4.3   **Job offers**

B.4.3.1   Jobs should be offered on the basis of the suitability of the candidates and not on the grounds of sex, race or trade union membership.

B.4.3.2   The terms of any job offer should not deter a prospective applicant of any sex, race or trade union position from accepting the job. The job offer should be the same as any other person might receive.

B.4.3.3   It is not discriminatory to ask non-EC citizens whether they have an appropriate work permit.

B.4.4   **Terms and conditions of employment**

Terms and conditions of employment and fringe benefits must not discriminate against sexes or races. Contractual terms and benefits affecting the sexes are dealt with under EqPA (see B.3), but terms and conditions of employment which discriminate between the races are dealt with under the RRA.

B.4.5   **Training**

B.4.5.1   Access to training must be available equally whatever the sex, race or trade union position of the employee, unless the employer is seeking to train up people of a particular sex or race who have not traditionally performed work of that type during the previous twelve months. Terms of access must be equal, and no training should be terminated early or be subject to any detriment on the ground of sex, race or trade union position. For example, it would not be discriminatory to train women to be bricklayers or to provide extra training for those who have been absent from work for a period because of family commitments.

B.4.5.2   Examples of legitimate positive training are:

B.4.5.2.1   Career counselling for women wishing to return to work.

B.4.5.2.2   Skills training where a comparatively small number of people doing the job in Great Britain or in the relevant area are of any one sex or race. Statistics regarding the number of people performing a job are obtainable from the Department of Employment, and before embarking upon any positive training the employer should check that the circumstances allow positive training.

Employers may obtain grants from the European Social Fund to give positive training. Applications for grants are handled by the Department of Employment.

B.4.6   **Promotion and transfer**

Access to transfer and promotion must be applied equally whatever the sex, race or trade union position of the individual.

B.4.7   **Pregnant women**

Any treatment of a woman who is ill as a result of pregnancy or any other gynaecological complaint should be the same as that which would have been given to any person suffering from an asexual complaint which would result in similar periods off work.

B.4.8   **Pension schemes**

Occupational pension schemes must not contain any discriminatory terms.

B.4.9   **Sexual harrassment**

Various forms of sexual harrassment may be discriminatory. Examples include:

B.4.9.1   Unwelcome sexual attention.

B.4.9.2   A suggestion that sexual activity or its refusal may help or hinder a career.

B.4.9.3   Sustained obscene or lewd language or behaviour.

B.4.9.4   The display of sexually suggestive material.

Sexual harrassment is unlawful if it causes an employee detriment, for example, to her health or promotion prospects, or genuinely causes her to resign or seek a transfer of employment. In serious cases, sexual harrassment could be a legitimate cause for constructive dismissal (see E.4.3).

B.4.10   **Victimisation**

Employers must not victimise anyone who has brought or might bring a claim for discrimination or is to be a witness in any such claim.

B.4.11   **Redundancy**

Criteria for selection for redundancy should not be discriminatory.

B.4.12   **Dismissal**

Dismissal on any ground should not be by reason of race, sex or trade union membership. For example, it would be discriminatory if any policy that spouses should not work together automatically resulted in the dismissal or transfer of the wife rather than the husband. It could also be discriminatory if two people were accused of an offence but only one, of a particular sex or race, was dismissed.

B.5   DEFENCES TO DISCRIMINATION CLAIMS

B.5.1   Treatment not discriminatory

If the employer can show that an individual would have received the same treatment, whatever the motive, despite his or her own sex or race or trade union membership, there will be no discrimination. De minimis differences, for example describing what clothing someone of any sex must wear, are normally ignored and are not sufficiently serious to warrant a finding of discrimination.

B.5.2   Genuine occupational qualification on the ground of sex

It is a defence to any claim of sex discrimination that the position requires a person of a particular sex, for example:

B.5.2.1   Physiology and authenticity in entertainment matters, for example models and actors.

B.5.2.2   Requirements of decency or privacy, for example lavatory attendants.

B.5.2.3   Jobs in a single-sex establishment such as a prison.

B.5.2.4   Work abroad which can only be done by a man, for example certain types of work in the Middle East.

B.5.2.5   A job which is one of two to be done by a married couple.

B.5.2.6   A job which requires personal services towards the welfare and education of others which can most effectively be done by a person of the same sex.

B.5.2.7   A job which is likely to involve the holder living in or working in a private home with a degree of physical or social contact with other persons living there or involving intimate details of such person's life, such as a private nurse or companion.

B.5.2.8   A job where the employee would have to live in, and there are no separate sleeping or toilet arrangements between the sexes.

B.5.3   **Genuine occupational qualification on ground of race**

It will be a defence to any claim for race discrimination that there is a genuine need for a position to be filled by a person of a particular race, for example:

B.5.3.1   To provide authenticity in entertainment (for example, acting).

B.5.3.2   Jobs requiring personal services towards the welfare of others which can most effectively be done by a person of a particular race (for example, community officers).

B.5.3.3   Jobs in establishments where it is necessary to maintain a particular ambience, for example in an ethnic bar or restaurant.

B.5.4   **Other exceptions**

There can be no claim for sex discrimination in the following cases:

B.5.4.1   Ministers of religion.

B.5.4.2   Arrangements regarding the provision of sports facilities.

B.5.4.3   Police.

B.5.4.4   Armed Forces.

B.5.4.5   Prison officers (although the blanket exception only applies to requirements that people should be of a particular height — for other exemptions see the general rule under B.5.2.3).

B.5.4.6   Special treatment afforded to women in connection with pregnancy and childbirth.

B.5.4.7   Some senior academic posts, e.g., where a University Dean must also be an Anglican minister.

B.5.5   **No vicarious responsibility**

If a discriminatory act has been carried out by an employee or agent of the employer, although the employer took such steps as were reasonably practicable to ensure that that act or type of act was proscribed, the employer itself will not be found guilty of discrimination. The employee or agent himself or herself may however be liable.

B.6   **BRINGING A COMPLAINT: RECOMMENDATIONS FOR EMPLOYEES**

B.6.1   The employee should either identify a male or person of different race treated differently or should show how, hypothetically, a member of the opposite sex or another race *would* have been treated differently in the relevant circumstances.

B.6.2   The employee should establish the material facts. In cases of indirect discrimination, the employee should obtain statistical evidence to show that a particular requirement disadvantages members of a particular race or sex. Statistical evidence may also be relevant in other areas.

B.6.3   The employee should identify to whom the complaint should be addressed. Employers are normally responsible or vicariously liable for the acts of their employees or agents provided they have not taken such steps as were reasonably practicable to prevent the act or type of act from being performed. Where acts have been carried out through an employee or agent, the employee should consider suing the individual as well, together with anyone else who has aided or abetted the discrimination.

B.6.4   **Equal Opportunities Commission/Commission for Racial Equality (EOC/CRE)**

B.6.4.1   Individuals who feel they may have been subject to discrimination may ask the EOC or the CRE either to conduct an official investigation on their behalf or to assist in the conduct of any claim.

B.6.4.2   If the EOC or the CRE gives notice that it intends to conduct a formal investigation, employers must supply all information requested. Fines are imposed for falsifying evidence. In addition, the employer should comply with any non-discrimination notice that may be sent following the investigation. An appeal against the notice must be made to an industrial tribunal within six weeks of the notice being served.

B.6.5   An employee may submit a Sex Discrimination Act or Race Relations Act questionnaire asking the employer to confirm or deny certain facts. The employer is not obliged to answer these questions but any failure to answer, or any inaccurate or evasive answers, may be taken into account by any industrial tribunal considering the issue of discrimination at a later date, and it may draw adverse inferences from such answers or failure to answer.

B.6.6   **Conciliation**

The employer may seek conciliation of the problem through ACAS.

B.6.7   **Industrial tribunal complaint**

Any complaint to the industrial tribunal must be brought within three months of the act complained of unless the tribunal thinks it just and equitable to extend the period. Continuing discrimination ends only when the practice ceases to be discriminatory. There is a distinction between a single act with continuing effects and the constant repetition of discriminatory acts.

B.6.8   **Remedies**

B.6.8.1   The tribunal may make a declaration of the rights of the parties.

B.6.8.2   The tribunal may make a recommendation that an employer should take a particular action (within a particular period) to obviate or reduce the adverse effect of discrimination. If this is not complied with, a further complaint can be made.

B.6.8.3   The tribunal may award compensation for losses flowing from discrimination, including losses for injury to feelings. In extreme cases, exemplary or aggravated damages may be awarded. Compensation cannot be awarded in indirect discrimination cases unless the employer intended the discrimination to occur, which is unusual.

B.7   **GENERAL RECOMMENDATIONS TO EMPLOYERS**

B.7.1   **Equal opportunities policy**

The employer should institute a policy which seeks to ensure that no discriminatory actions are conducted, and also which provides a mechanism for dealing with any query or complaint. The Equal Opportunities Commission provides a model code, if necessary. The policy should, however, deal with the following:

B.7.1.1   A statement of the commitment of the employer to equal opportunities and to removing barriers to equal opportunities.

B.7.1.2   Definitions of direct and indirect discrimination, victimisation and harrassment.

B.7.1.3   A statement of the standards to be followed together with examples of inappropriate behaviour.

B.7.1.4   The names of the officers responsible for implementing the policy.

B.7.1.5   An obligation on all employees to adhere to the policy, with a statement that failure to do so could be a disciplinary offence.

B.7.1.6   Procedures for dealing with any complaint.

B.7.1.7   Details of methods used to maintain and review the procedures.

B.7.2   Practical steps

Employers should take all practical steps to prevent their employees from discriminating against others, for example:

B.7.2.1   Employers should make sure everyone knows of the existence and contents of the equal opportunities policy.

B.7.2.2   Training should be provided for all those involved in recruitment such as personnel officers, interviewers and receptionists, together with any managers involved.

B.7.2.3   Those given responsibility for implementing the equal opportunities policy should regularly check that it is being complied with, for example by collating relevant statistics.

B.7.3   Job evaluation scheme

Employers should consider whether it is appropriate for them to conduct a job evaluation scheme. The advantage of such a scheme is that, provided that it has not been set up following discriminatory instructions, and it is implemented and complied with, it becomes extremely difficult for any employee to complain that a contractual term implemented in compliance with the scheme is discriminatory. The disadvantage is that the scheme is relatively expensive to institute, and, once carried out, may only be disregarded if there are new circumstances which would justify departing from its terms.

B.7.4   Employers should seek dispensation from the quota system in the Disabled Persons (Employment) Act if the quota is unreasonably high in the particular circumstances, for example because there is an insufficient number of disabled people to fulfil the 3 per cent quota.

C   Maternity Rights

The statutory provisions regarding maternity rights are inordinately complex. Employees have differing maternity rights in accordance with the length of their employment. Rights available include the right to paid time off for antenatal care, the right not to be dismissed or made redundant because of pregnancy or a reason connected with pregnancy, the right to receive maternity pay and the right to return to work.

Antenatal care

All employees are entitled to be paid at their normal hourly rates to attend antenatal care so long as, for the second and each subsequent visit, they supply their employers on request with a medical certificate of pregnancy and an appointment card. Employers must not unreasonably refuse this request, and if they do so the employee is able to apply to the industrial tribunal, within three months of the relevant appointment, for an order that the employer pays the employee money in lieu of the time spent attending antenatal care.

Right not to be dismissed

Employees' rights not to be dismissed because they are pregnant or for a reason connected with pregnancy arise only in the same circumstances as a right not to be unfairly dismissed. In other words, employees have to have at least two years' prior continuous employment (or five years' prior continuous employment if working between 8 and 16 hours per week) before the right accrues, and only those in qualifying occupations can claim the right (see E.3.1 and E.3.2).

The courts put a wide interpretation on a dismissal connected with pregnancy. Examples include not only dismissal because of pregnancy itself, but also a dismissal because an employee has taken too much sick leave as a result of her pregnancy, because she has a pregnancy-related illness or because she is ill as a result of a miscarriage.

There is an exemption to the general rule if it is medically or legally impossible for the employee to continue in her job during her pregnancy, and there is no suitable alternative position available which the employee can be offered on terms not substantially less favourable than under her old position. In these circumstances, an employer may dismiss an employee, but if she has worked for the appropriate time periods she will still be entitled to maternity pay and to the right to return to work following the pregnancy.

An employee who is unfairly dismissed because she is pregnant or for reasons connected with pregnancy is entitled to the same remedies as any other employee who is unfairly dismissed.

Statutory maternity pay (SMP)

Employees who have been employed for less than 26 weeks immediately before the 14th week before their expected week of confinement (EWC) are entitled only to receive a maternity allowance from the DSS. All other employees must be paid SMP by their employer. This payment is treated as a normal taxable sum, and tax and national insurance should be deducted from it. Employers can recover the SMP paid (together with the relevant national insurance supplement) by deducting the payments from subsequent payments of national insurance which the employer is required to make in respect of all his employees.

The maximum period during which SMP is payable is 18 weeks. For employees who have been employed for at least two years by the 14th week before the EWC, the first six weeks of SMP are paid at 90 per cent of the employees' normal weekly earnings. For those who have not been employed this long, and for all subsequent weeks, SMP is paid at a fixed 'lower rate' which, from 6 April 1992 is £46.30 per week.

SMP is only payable in respect of any weeks during which the employee is not actually working. Further, the employee is only entitled to the maximum of 18 weeks' SMP if she stops working between the eleventh and sixth weeks before her confinement. If she works after the sixth week before her confinement, the number of weeks' SMP she receives will be reduced by the number of weeks she works after the sixth week before the EWC. Employees who are fairly dismissed as a result of pregnancy because it would be physically or legally impossible to continue to employ them are entitled to SMP even if their employment ceases before the eleventh week before their EWC. The level of SMP may be subject to challenge under European law if it is less than the contractual sick pay to which the employee would have been entitled.

Right to return to work

Employees who have been employed for at least two years before the beginning of the eleventh week before their EWC are entitled, should they so wish, to return to work. There are stringent conditions which the employee must fulfil before she is able to exercise her right to return. The employer and the employee may by contract vary these provisions, but they can only do so to make the terms *more favourable* to the employee. If the employee has a contractual entitlement to return to work and any element of that contract places upon her more stringent conditions than statute would, the statutory provisions are deemed to replace those conditions which are more stringent.

The right to return to work exists even if, before the proposed return date, the employee has been unfairly dismissed for a reason connected with pregnancy. However, if the employee chooses to exercise her right to return in those circumstances, she must refund to the employer, on request, any redundancy payment or compensation payment previously made to her as a result of the dismissal.

Generally, the right to return to work must be exercised within 29 weeks of the actual week of confinement. There are only three circumstances when this period may be extended: the employer can, for good reason, extend the return date by a period of up to four weeks; the employee may extend the return date for a period of up to four weeks, if prevented by reason of ill health from returning on the date previously notified as the return date; and the period may be extended if it would be unreasonable for the employee to return to work within the 29-week period because of an 'interruption' at work. To qualify, this interruption must be in the nature of a lay-off or industrial action, and should relate to the employment itself and not to any special circumstances involving only the employee.

If the employee has satisfied the notice requirements to enable her to exercise the right to return to work, the employer must offer the employee either her old job back (with her pay, seniority and pension rights at least as good as she had before) or he must offer her a suitable employment which is (a) compatible with her skills, qualifications and status, (b) appropriate for her to perform in the circumstances, and (c) on terms not substantially less favourable than those which applied to her old job. If such a position is not offered, the employee is treated as unfairly dismissed. If the employee's old job is redundant and there are no suitable alternative positions, the employee will be deemed to have been continuously employed throughout the period of her confinement until her notified date of return, and is then entitled to a redundancy payment.

C.1 ENTITLEMENTS FOR DIFFERING LENGTHS OF SERVICE

C.1.1 Ascertain the employee's expected week of confinement (EWC). A week for these purposes runs from Sunday to Saturday inclusive. The employee will then have the rights set out in the table on p. 53, depending upon how long she has been employed before her EWC.

C.1.2   In addition, women continuously employed (or deemed continuously employed through their absence from work as a result of pregnancy) for more than two years and for 16 hours or more per week, or for more than five years working between 8 and 16 hours per week, have the right not to be dismissed because they are pregnant or for a reason connected with pregnancy. (See Appendix.)

C.2   ANTENATAL CARE

C.2.1   First appointment

Is this the first appointment for the employee? If so, the employee is entitled to be paid at her normal hourly rate to attend an antenatal appointment, unless the employer reasonably refuses to do so.

C.2.2   Subsequent appointments

Is it the employee's second or subsequent appointment? If so, the employee must supply the employer, if the employer so requests, with a certificate of pregnancy signed by a doctor or midwife, together with an appropriate appointment card.

C.2.3   Alternative arrangements

Could the employee normally make arrangements to attend antenatal care outside her normal working hours? If so, it may be reasonable for the employer to refuse the employee paid time off to attend antenatal care.

C.2.4   Refusal

Has the employer unreasonably refused the employee's request? If so, the employee may apply to the industrial tribunal within three months of the appointment date for an Order that the employer pay her what she would have earnt during the time taken attending the appointment, including travelling and waiting time.

C.3   DISMISSAL

C.3.1   Unfair dismissal

Generally, it will be automatically unfair to dismiss an employee because she is pregnant or for any reason connected with pregnancy if:

C.3.1.1   she has been continuously employed for at least two years, working 16 hours or more per week; or

C.3.1.2   she has been continuously employed for five years, working 8 hours or more per week.

For continuity of employment provisions see E.3.2. (See Appendix.)

C.3.2   Definition

Pregnancy or a reason connected with pregnancy includes:

C.3.2.1   Pregnancy itself.

C.3.2.2   The fact that the employee has taken too much sick leave as a result of being pregnant.

C.3.2.3   A pregnancy-related illness.

C.3.2.4   A miscarriage.

C.3.2.5   The fact that an employer will have to pay the employee statutory maternity pay (SMP) or a contractual maternity payment when she is absent from work.

Any dismissal or selection for redundancy on these or similar grounds will be automatically unfair, except in the circumstances described in C.3.3.

C.3.3   Fair dismissals

The only grounds relating to pregnancy where an employee may lawfully be dismissed are that:

C.3.3.1   It is medically impossible for the employee adequately to carry out her duties because she is pregnant; for example, because her pregnancy is creating a medical or physical condition over and above the normal side-effects of pregnancy, such as anxiety or anaemia, which makes it impossible for her to work properly; or

C.3.3.2   It is against the law for the employee to continue to perform her normal duties. The main legal exemptions relate to health and safety provisions in particular industries. (See Appendix.)

In these circumstances, if the employer has a suitable alternative position for the pregnant employee, on terms which are not substantially less favourable than those she enjoyed under her old post, he must offer it to the employee. He does not have to create such a position. If such a position does not exist, then the employer may terminate the employee's contract.

If the employee's contract is lawfully terminated in accordance with C.3.3.1 and C.3.3.2 the employee nevertheless has the right, provided that she has worked for the appropriate periods of time, to SMP.

C.3.4   **Synopsis of dismissal provisions**

C.3.4.1   Has the employee been employed for two years or more full time or five years or more part time (see C.3.1)? (See Appendix.)

C.3.4.1.1   If not, the employee may be dismissed for a reason connected with pregnancy, although this may amount to discrimination in European law.

C.3.4.1.2   If she has, she can only be dismissed if it is medically or legally impossible for her to continue working.

C.3.4.2   If the employer reasonably suspects that it is medically impossible for the employee to continue carrying out her duties, he should:

C.3.4.2.1   Obtain appropriate medical evidence.

C.3.4.2.2   If medical evidence confirms the suspicions, see if there are any alternative posts which the employee can safely fill. If they exist, they should be offered to the employee. If the employee refuses the offer, or if there is no alternative, the employee may be dismissed.

C.3.4.3   If it is legally impossible for the employee to continue carrying out her duties the employer should see if there are any alternative posts which the employee can safely fill. If they exist, they should be offered to the employee. If the employee refuses the offer, or if there is no alternative, the employee may be dismissed. (See Appendix.)

C.3.4.4   If an employee with appropriate length of service thinks that she has been unfairly dismissed as a result of pregnancy:

C.3.4.4.1   She should bring a claim in the industrial tribunal within three months of the dismissal. If the employee has validly exercised her right to return to work, but is not allowed by the employer to do so, the deemed date of dismissal will be the notified date of return.

C.3.4.4.2   If she wants to seek to exercise her right to return to work she should still fulfill all the relevant conditions (see C.5).

C.3.4.5   Even if the employee is dismissed, if she has worked for the relevant periods she will still be entitled to SMP and to the right to return to work. (See Appendix.)

C.4   STATUTORY MATERNITY PAY (SMP)

Depending on the employee's length of service, she may be entitled to SMP (see C.4.1 and C.4.2). The periods for which SMP is payable are set out in C.4.3, and the amount in C.4.4.

C.4.1   Entitlement

An employee who has been employed for less than 26 weeks immediately before the 14th week before her EWC is entitled to receive a maternity allowance but not SMP. The maternity allowance is paid by the DSS. Other employees are generally entitled to SMP. (See Appendix.)

C.4.2   Conditions

The conditions which must be met before SMP is payable are that:

C.4.2.1   The employee must have been employed for at least 26 weeks immediately before the 14th week before her EWC whether or not she has actually been working throughout this period; or

C.4.2.2   the employee *would* have been employed for at least 26 weeks immediately before the 14th week before her EWC (whether or not she has actually been working throughout this period) had she not been dismissed for being medically or legally incapable of continuing to work (see C.3.3).

C.4.2.3   The employee must when she worked normally have had average earnings above the national insurance contributions lower earnings limit.

C.4.2.4   The employee must give her employer 21 days' notice of her intention to be absent because of pregnancy or confinement. This notice must be given in writing if the employer so requests. If it is not reasonably practicable for 21 days' notice to be given, the employee must give the employer notification as soon as it is reasonably practicable for her to do so.

C.4.2.5   The employee must provide the employer with evidence of her pregnancy and EWC. Appropriate evidence includes a certificate from a doctor or midwife.

C.4.2.6 The employee should not be working during any week when SMP is being paid. (See Appendix.)

C.4.3 **Period of SMP payment**

C.4.3.1 The maximum statutory period during which SMP is payable is 18 weeks.

C.4.3.2 Does the employee stop working during or before the sixth week before her EWC and remain out of work for at least 18 weeks thereafter? If so she is entitled to SMP for 18 weeks.

C.4.3.3 Does the employee stop work after the sixth week before her EWC? If so, the maximum period of her SMP is reduced by the number of weeks she has worked after the sixth week before her EWC.

C.4.3.4 Does the employee return to work before the end of her maximum permitted SMP period? If so, SMP will cease to be payable on her return to work.

C.4.4 **Amount of SMP**

C.4.4.1 Has the employee been continuously employed for more than 26 weeks but less than two years (whether or not actually working during the period) immediately before the 14th week before her EWC?

If so, the employee is entitled to SMP at the lower rate (£46.30 per week from 6 April 1992).

C.4.4.2 Has the employee been employed for at least two years (whether or not actually working during the period) immediately before the 14th week before her EWC?

If so, the employee is entitled to receive SMP at 90 per cent of her normal weekly earnings for the first six weeks of her absence, and to receive SMP at the lower rate (£46.30 per week from 6 April 1992) for each subsequent week.

C.4.4.3 Has the employee been lawfully dismissed as a result of her pregnancy, as described in C.3.3 above?

In these cases, for the purposes of assessing whether or not SMP is payable, she should be treated as if she were still in employment.

C.4.4.4   SMP is treated as if it were the normal income of an employee. Tax and national insurance should be deducted from it, and the employer must account to the Inland Revenue for employer's and employee's national insurance contributions.

C.4.5   General considerations

C.4.5.1   Has the employer failed to pay SMP? If so, the employee may request the reasons for this refusal and, if not satisfied, may refer the issue to an adjudication officer. Failure to pay SMP which is due is an offence.

C.4.5.2   The employer must keep records of SMP payments for three years.

C.4.5.3   The employer may recover any SMP payments made by deducting the amount of the payments (including the employers' national insurance contributions, in respect of the SMP) from national insurance contributions he makes on behalf of his employees in general.

C.4.5.4   The employee must notify the employer if she accepts employment elsewhere. The employer's liability to pay SMP to the employee ceases immediately upon the employee taking up such new employment. Any overpayment can be recovered from the employee.

C.5   RIGHT TO RETURN TO WORK

C.5.1   Conditions

The employee must satisfy all the following conditions before she is entitled to return to work:

C.5.1.1   She must have been employed under a contract of employment for at least two years before the beginning of the eleventh week before the EWC; or

C.5.1.2   she would have been employed under a contract of employment (whether or not it required her to work for more or less than 8 hours per week) for at least two years by the beginning of the eleventh week before her EWC, but has not been only because she was fairly dismissed because she was medically or legally incapable of continuing to work (see C.3.3).

C.5.1.3   The employee must not have resigned from her employment before going on maternity leave.

C.5.1.4   The employee must notify the employer in writing at least 21 days before her absence on maternity leave of (a) the fact she will be absent from work wholly or partly because of her pregnancy, (b) her EWC, and (c) the fact that she intends to return. The notice period may be reduced if it is not reasonably practicable for the employee to have given the employer such notice, but in those circumstances notice must be given as soon as is practicable.

C.5.1.5   If the employee has been fairly dismissed because she is physically or legally incapable of continuing to work (see C.3.3), she must notify the employer before the dismissal takes effect or as soon as possible thereafter of her intention to return to work. The notification should be in writing if the employer so requests.

C.5.1.6   The employee must provide, if so requested by her employer, a medical certificate stating her EWC.

C.5.1.7   If the employer, after at least 7 weeks have elapsed from the beginning of the EWC or the actual birth itself (see Appendix), requests the employee in writing to give written confirmation of her intention to return to work, the employee must comply with this request within 2 weeks or (if this is not reasonably practicable) as soon as is practicable thereafter. The employer's request must be accompanied by a written statement that the employee will lose her rights unless she replies within two weeks of receipt of the letter or (if this is not reasonably practicable) as soon as is practicable thereafter.

C.5.1.8   The employee must notify her employer in writing of her intention to return at least 21 days in advance of her 'notified date of return'.

C.5.1.9   Unless legitimately extended (see C.5.3), the employee must return to work not more than 29 weeks after the birth of her child. This period of 29 weeks means 29 pay weeks after the pay week during which the birth took place.

These provisions need not be followed if the employer has agreed that the employee shall be subject to less stringent requirements before she may return to work, or that she may in any event return to work after her pregnancy. If no such agreement exists, and if the employee has not complied with all the conditions set out above, she will not be entitled to return to work.

C.5.2   No right to return

In certain circumstances, even if the employee fulfils the conditions set out in C.5.1, she will still have no right to return to work. These are:

C.5.2.1   If, just before the employee's absence on maternity leave, the employer employed five or fewer employees (including the pregnant employee) and if, when the time comes for the employee's reinstatement, it is not reasonably practicable for the employer or any associated employer to offer the employee her old job back or a suitable and appropriate alternative.

C.5.2.2   If it is not reasonably practicable for the employer to permit the employee to return and the employer has offered the employee suitable employment (which is compatible with her skills, qualifications and status) which it is appropriate for her to do on terms which are not substantially less favourable than those which applied in her old job.

If such an alternative job is not offered, the employee will have been unfairly dismissed.

C.5.2.3   If the employee's old job is redundant and the employer does not have any suitable alternative employment.

If no alternative job exists, the employee is treated as having been continuously employed until her notified date of return, and following this date is entitled to a redundancy payment, based upon continuous service until her notified date of return, in the normal way.

C.5.2.4   If the employee is in overseas employment or the police service.

C.5.3   Postponing the return date

The period by which the employee must have returned to work after pregnancy to keep alive her rights may be extended in only three circumstances:

C.5.3.1   If the employee is unwell, she may extend her return date for up to four pay weeks after her notified date of return. She must have produced a medical certificate as to her disability before her notified date of return. Only one extension can be obtained.

C.5.3.2   The employer may delay the employee's return for a period up to four weeks beyond the notified day of return, provided he has good reason to do so. The employer must give the employee notice, before the notified date of return, of the reasons for the delay and of the proposed return date.

C.5.3.3   If there is an 'interruption' in work, such as a lay-off or industrial action, making it unreasonable for the employee to return to work by the end of the 29th week, the employer should inform the employee, before the notified date of return or the end of the 29th week, of that interruption in work and the employee must in due course notify the employer of her proposed revised return date which should not be more than 28 days after the interruption ends.

C.5.4   Position on return

Unless it is not reasonably practicable for the employer to permit the employee to return (in which case see C.5.2), the employee's position on return should be:

C.5.4.1   Her pay, seniority and pension rights must be the same as or better than those applying before her maternity leave.

C.5.4.2   While her duties may change, her job package on the whole must be as favourable or more favourable than the one applying before her maternity leave.

C.5.4.3   Her employment is deemed to be continuous, for all purposes, throughout the period of her pregnancy.

C.5.5   General comments

C.5.5.1   The right to return to work still exists even if an employee was unfairly dismissed during her absence on maternity leave, although if she does return she must repay to the employer, if requested so to do, any redundancy pay or compensation payment she has received in respect of such dismissal.

C.5.5.2   If the employee fulfils all the conditions for her return to work but the employer refuses to allow her to return, and if the reason for this refusal is connected with the employee's pregnancy, the dismissal will be automatically unfair. The dismissal can only be fair if the reason for dismissal is not to do with pregnancy, but is within one of the categories of fair dismissals (see E.5.1 and E.5.2) and the employer has followed the normal procedures.

ENTITLEMENT TO RIGHTS

Minimum length of service	Time off for antenatal care	Right not to be the subject of sex discrimination	Maternity payment rate during absent weeks	Right to return to work
Less than 26 weeks immediately before *14th week* before EWC	Yes	Yes	Maternity allowance from DSS (see Appendix — C.4.1)	No
Between 26 weeks and two years immediately before *14th week* before EWC	Yes	Yes	SMP for up to 18 weeks, paid by employer, at lower fixed rate (see Appendix — C.4.2)	No
Two years or more before *11th week* before EWC	Yes	Yes	SMP for up to 18 weeks, paid by employer, at lower fixed rate (see Appendix — C.4.2)	Yes
Two years or more before *14th week* before EWC	Yes	Yes	SMP for six weeks at 90 per cent of normal weekly earnings plus SMP for the balance (up to 12 weeks) at lower fixed rate	Yes

D Industrial Action

No employee in England has a right to withdraw his labour with impunity. Any industrial action, whether it involves only a refusal to comply with some contractual requirements or a complete withdrawal of labour, is a breach of the individual's contract of employment. In principle, any third party who encourages employees to take industrial action, whether by breaching their employment contracts or by forcing a breach of a contract which their employer has with a customer or supplier, commits the tort of inducing a breach of contract. Other so-called 'industrial torts' include interference with the employers' business by unlawful means, intimidation and conspiracy.

In certain circumstances, independent trade unions may be immune from liability if they commit an industrial tort. The circumstances have been gradually narrowed by legislation during recent years. First, any industrial action encouraged by a trade union must fall within the 'golden formula' that is it must be in contemplation or furtherance of a trade dispute. Second, no industrial action can be taken unless it is supported by a majority vote in a properly held ballot. Third, the first element in any industrial action must take place within 28 days of the announcement of the result of the strike ballot. Fourth, even if employed officials of a trade union have not authorised or endorsed industrial action, the union may still be regarded as responsible if the action has been authorised or endorsed by any committee of the union or any of the officials of the union (whether employed by it or not), and in those circumstances the union can only escape liability by repudiating the industrial action. If a dispute concerning a closed shop is one of the reasons for industrial action, then the trade union immunity will automatically cease, whatever other reasons there may be for the action.

A dispute is only a dispute within the golden formula if it relates to an issue between an employer and his own employees for a legitimate reason. The only form of 'secondary action' which is permitted, and even then only in limited circumstances, is picketing. Thus, an employee of one employer cannot 'black' work which would normally have been done by a separate employer (of even an associated company) which is in dispute with some of its employees.

The remedies available to an employer in respect of any industrial action are the normal remedies which would be available upon commission of any breach of contract or tort. Thus, for example, employees may be dismissed for committing a repudiatory breach of contract, or they can be sued for damages flowing from the breach. They cannot, however, be forced back to work since it is against public policy to require a person to work against his or her will. A trade union can be sued, on occasions where the trade union immunity does not apply, for damages for inducement to others to breach their contracts, subject to certain limits depending upon the size of the union's membership; the employer can also apply for an injunction restraining the trade union and its officials from encouraging any industrial action and may move for sequestration of union assets if the union fails to comply.

D.1   WHAT IS A LEGITIMATE TRADE DISPUTE?

D.1.1   Unions can only seek the benefit of any trade union immunity if the industrial action which they are encouraging is within the 'golden formula' of categories of trade dispute. Those trade disputes must be between an employer and his own workers. The term 'workers' means not only employees but also self-employed people who have agreed personally to perform any work or services for the employer, where the employer is not a client. The definition therefore includes casual workers.

D.1.2   Legitimate trade disputes are those which relate wholly or mainly to one of the following issues:

D.1.2.1   Terms and conditions of employment.

D.1.2.2   Physical conditions in which any worker is required to work.

D.1.2.3   The engagement, non-engagement, termination or suspension of employment or the duties of employment of one or more workers.

D.1.2.4   Demarcation disputes.

D.1.2.5   General disputes regarding allocation of work and duties of employment.

D.1.2.6   Disciplinary matters.

D.1.2.7   A worker's membership or non-membership of a trade union.

D.1.2.8   Facilities for officials of trade unions.

D.1.2.9   Machinery for negotiation or consultation.

D.1.2.10   Recognition disputes.

D.1.3   Any dispute which has, as one of its reasons, a conflict concerning a closed shop can never be a legitimate trade dispute and the industrial action will automatically be unlawful.

D.2   THE BALLOT PAPER

D.2.1   If the trade union immunity is to apply, industrial action must be supported by a validly conducted ballot. The following should be considered:

D.2.1.1   Does the ballot paper state, without qualification, 'if you take part in a strike or other industrial action, you may be in breach of your contract of employment'? and

D.2.1.2   Does the ballot paper ask a question, requiring the person to answer yes or no, whether the individual is prepared to take part in a strike? and/or (as the case may be): Does the ballot paper ask a question, requiring the person answering it to say yes or no, whether the individual is prepared to take part in action short of a strike? and

D.2.1.3   Does the ballot paper specify who is authorised for the purposes of Section 7 of the Employment Act 1990 to call upon members to take part in the industrial action? (See Appendix.)

                  If any of these elements is missing, the ballot is invalid.

D.2.2   Does any message on the ballot paper detract from any of the required statements? If so, the ballot is invalid.

D.2.3   The ballot/voting

D.2.3.1   Who is entitled to vote in the ballot? It should be only those members of the trade union employed by the employer with whom there is a dispute whom it is reasonable at the time of the ballot for the chapel/union to believe will be asked to take part in industrial action.

D.2.3.2   Is there anyone who is entitled to vote who is not given the opportunity to vote?

D.2.3.3   Is there anyone who was not given the opportunity to vote — probably because he is not in the relevant area — who is nevertheless being induced to go out on strike?

If there are several such persons, bearing in mind the total number entitled to vote, the ballot is likely to be invalid. If one or two people are inadvertently missed off this is unlikely to invalidate the ballot.

D.2.4   **Conduct of ballot** (See Appendix.)

D.2.4.1   When and where does the ballot take place?

D.2.4.2   How are the ballot papers distributed — by post or by hand?

D.2.4.3   Is the ballot secret?

D.2.4.4   Is any voter required to incur direct cost in, for example, having to pay to enter a hall to vote or having to travel to the voting place?

If the ballot is not conducted secretly, with all potential voters given a reasonable opportunity to vote, it is likely to be invalid.

D.2.5   Has the union informed all persons voting in the ballot of the total number of votes cast, the number of 'yes' votes, the number of 'no' votes and the number of spoiled papers?

It should announce these figures to those entitled to vote in the ballot. (See Appendix.)

D.2.6   What was the result of the ballot? Was there a majority in favour of any of the questions specified on the ballot paper? If not, any industrial action thereafter will be unlawful.

D.2.7   Has there been an official call for industrial action before the ballot was held? If so the action will be unlawful on the part of the union.

D.3   **INDUSTRIAL ACTION**

D.3.1   Who called for industrial action? Is it the person who is specified on the ballot paper (see D.2.1.3)? If not, the action will be unlawful.

D.3.2   When does the call for industrial action take place? Has there been any authorisation or endorsement of industrial action before the date of the ballot? If so, the ballot will be invalid.

D.3.3   Is industrial action threatened or taking place without the sanction of a valid ballot? If so, and if it is action by a union official and not repudiated by the union, either all individuals taking industrial action may be dismissed (although all must be treated equally

from the date of dismissal for a period of three months, in that
there must be no selective re-engagement in this period) or the
union and others calling the action may be restrained by
injunction from pursuing action.

D.3.4   Has the industrial action been repudiated by the principal
executive committee or the general secretary of the union both to
the chapel/FOC, and to the union members, and to the employer?
For repudiation to be effective, the union must give written notice
of repudiation as quickly as possible to those authorising the strike
and also to every member of the union who might take part in the
strike and his/her employer, including the statement 'your union
has repudiated any call for industrial action to which this notice
relates and will give no support to such action. If you are dismissed
while taking unofficial action, you will have no right to complain
of unfair dismissal.' If the action has been called in the union's
name, is not repudiated, and is unlawful, the union will be
responsible for any damage suffered as a result of the action. If the
action is unofficial, or has been repudiated by the union, the
employer may dismiss any individuals taking industrial action,
and is not obliged to treat all such individuals equally in order to
avoid applications for unfair dismissal.

D.4   **EMPLOYERS' POSSIBLE REMEDIES**

D.4.1   If employees are in breach of their contracts of employment, either
because they go on strike or because they commit a material
breach of their contracts of employment, such as refusing to
perform duties which they are contractually obliged to perform
(and in this context a work-to-rule may still be a breach of an
implied contractual term that employees should co-operate with
the employer), the employer has the following remedies (see
Appendix also):

D.4.1.1   He may refuse to pay employees for the period when they have
been taking industrial action. If an employee takes industrial
action in the form of refusing to perform only one of several tasks,
and the employer makes it clear he does not accept partial
performance of duties, the employer may still refuse to pay the
employee any pay for the entire duration of the industrial action
unless the industrial action represents a specific identifiable period
of non-work, in which case pay should be deducted only for that
period. If the employer indicates he will accept partial performance of the contract he should pay the employee a rateable
proportion of the normal wages covering those duties which the
employee has actually performed.

D.4.1.2   He may sue employees for the losses which he has suffered as a result of breaches of their contracts of employment. This may be difficult to quantify, and any such action would not assist harmonious industrial relations once the dispute has ended. Further, the individuals sued may not have enough funds to be worth suing.

D.4.1.3   If the dispute is one which has been authorised by the relevant trade union, he may dismiss those employees taking industrial action. The employer must, in such a case however, treat all employees taking industrial action in the same way. Employees who are absent from work through sickness or on holiday should not be dismissed unless the employer is satisfied that they are taking part in the industrial action.

D.4.1.3.1   In respect of employees who are sick, employers should, if only a few people are sick, visit each employee's home during normal working hours to ascertain whether or not the employee would, if well, be on strike. If a substantial number of employees are sick, the employer may write to the employees. The letter should ask the employees whether, if they had not been sick, they would have worked normally on specified dates, and whether the individual is prepared to undertake to return to work normally immediately following recovery. These questions should require the answer, yes or no. If either of the questions is answered in the negative this would be sufficient to constitute 'taking part' in industrial action.

D.4.1.3.2   In respect of those individuals on holiday, if they can easily be contacted, they should be visited to ascertain whether or not they would, if not on holiday, be on strike. If there are a large number of them, they should be written to and asked whether, if they had not been on holiday, they would have worked normally on a specified date and whether they are prepared to undertake to return to work normally as soon as their holiday period ends. The individuals should be required to answer yes or no to both questions. If either of the questions is answered in the negative, this would be sufficient to constitute 'taking part' in industrial action. If individuals cannot be contacted, action should not be taken against them unless and until they have demonstrated, following their return, an intention to take part in industrial action.

             In these circumstances, because the employees are in material breach of their contracts of employment, the individuals dismissed have no right to money in lieu of notice, or to complain that they have been unfairly dismissed, unless some (but not all) of their number have not been dismissed or some are reinstated within three months of their dismissal. If any employee has been re-engaged within three months, any employees not re-engaged will be able to complain that they have been unfairly dismissed.

D.4.1.4   If the industrial action is unofficial, because it has not been authorised or endorsed by a relevant trade union or because a trade union has repudiated the action at least one working day earlier, the employer may select for dismissal some only of those employees taking industrial action. In those circumstances, dismissed employees have no right to money in lieu of notice or to claim that they have been unfairly dismissed.

D.4.2   The employer may consider taking the following steps against a trade union which is not able to take advantage of the trade union immunities. These circumstances arise where the dispute is not a legitimate trade dispute within the golden formula or where a ballot has not been conducted or has been improperly conducted, and in each case the trade union has either authorised or endorsed the industrial action, or has refused to repudiate any industrial action called for by any committee or official of the union (whether employed or not, so including a shop steward). If the industrial action involves any employees breaching their contracts of employment, or any interference with the employer's business by unlawful means or conspiracy to do so, the employer may:

D.4.2.1   Seek an injunction against the union restraining breaches.

D.4.2.2   Claim damages against the union for any losses proved to have been suffered by the employer as a result of the industrial action. The maximum sum of damages which can be awarded on any one claim against the union depends upon the number of members the union has:

D.4.2.2.1 If the union has fewer than 5,000 members, the maximum is £10,000.

D.4.2.2.2 If the union has between 5,000 and 24,999 members, the maximum is £50,000.

D.4.2.2.3 If the union has between 25,000 and 99,999 members, the maximum is £125,000.

D.4.2.2.4 If the union has 100,000 or more members, the maximum is £250,000.

D.5 **PICKETING**

The general rule is that all secondary action is prohibited. The sole exception to this rule is picketing, which is the only possible form of legitimate secondary industrial action, but even so the manner in which pickets can be conducted is severely limited.

D.5.1 **Criminal offences**

If an employer believes that any criminal offence is being or is about to be committed, the employer should contact the police to request them to take appropriate preventative action. Pickets may be guilty of the following crimes:

D.5.1.1 Obstructing the highway, by wilfully obstructing free passage along a public highway or pavement.

D.5.1.2 Obstructing a police constable in the execution of his duty.

D.5.1.3 Assault, provided the individual has the capacity to carry into effect an intention to commit some physical injury, however slight.

D.5.1.4 Offences under the Public Order Act 1986. These occur when an individual makes (orally, in writing or via pictures) threatening or abusive or insulting comments or actions towards another with the intention or the likely consequence that the individual believes he is likely to be the subject of immediate unlawful violence.

D.5.1.5 Unlawful assembly, where three or more people use or threaten violence as a result of which people might fear for their personal safety.

D.5.1.6 Affray and riot.

D.5.1.7 Public nuisance, for example by obstructing the public in the exercise or enjoyment of a right of way.

D.5.1.8 Offences under the Conspiracy and Protection of Property Act 1875 including:

D.5.1.8.1 Using violence towards or intimidating another.

D.5.1.8.2 Persistently following another from place to place.

D.5.1.8.3 Hiding any tools, clothes or other property owned or used by other people or depriving them or hindering them in their use.

D.5.1.8.4   Watching or besetting a person's residence or place of employment, or the approach to either place.

D.5.1.8.5   Following another person with two or more others in a disorderly manner in or through any street or road, in each case without legal authority.

D.5.1.9   Refusing to obey conditions imposed on a public assembly.

D.5.2   Civil wrongs

In addition, pickets may be found to have committed civil wrongs including:

D.5.2.1   trespass to the employer's property;

D.5.2.2   interference with contracts to which the employer is a party (for example, by preventing employers fulfilling their contracts, preventing employees from entering work, or preventing suppliers delivering supplies to the employer); or

D.5.2.3   private nuisance (for example by blocking an access route to an employer's premises).

D.5.3   Lawful pickets

Even if those picketing commit no crime or civil wrongs as set out in D.5.1 and D.5.2, a picket is only lawful in the following circumstances:

D.5.3.1   The only people who should be on a picket are workers picketing at or near their own place of work, or trade union officials accompanying their members. If employees work at more than one place of work or if it is impossible for them to picket at that place, they can picket the administrative headquarters of their employer. A person dismissed during the industrial dispute in question may picket his former place of work.

D.5.3.2   The only activities pickets can lawfully conduct are peacefully to obtain or communicate information or peacefully to persuade any person to work or abstain from working.

D.5.3.3   There is no specific restriction on the number of people at any picket. A mass picket is generally regarded as an obstruction of the highway or intimidation. The Department of Employment's Code of Practice recommends that in general there should be no more than six pickets at any entrance.

D.5.4   **Summary and consequences**

In general, pickets may not:

D.5.4.1   Threaten or intimidate any individual.

D.5.4.2   Obstruct the entrance to the employer's premises.

D.5.4.3   Trespass upon the employer's premises.

D.5.4.4   Obstruct the path of any vehicle seeking to enter the employer's premises.

D.5.4.5   Do more than seek peacefully to obtain or communicate information or persuade people not to work normally.

If any picket is not conducted properly in accordance with D.5.2 or D.5.3, employers can seek an injunction banning any picket other than one restricted to say, six people acting peacefully. The injunction may be directed against any union or individual which or who is authorising or endorsing an unlawful picket and against any individuals taking part in an unlawful picket.

D.6   **INJUNCTIONS**

D.6.1   It will be necessary for the employer to demonstrate to the court, by affidavit evidence, the following facts:

D.6.1.1   For industrial action injunctions:

D.6.1.1.1   The nature of the industrial action taken, and a brief history of the events leading up to the union's involvement in those events.

D.6.1.1.2   Whether the industrial action is within the golden formula.

D.6.1.1.3   Whether the ballot has been properly held. The employer has no legal right to a copy of the ballot paper or to details of the ballot result, although the relevant Code of Practice states that the union should respond positively, and in writing when so requested, to a request from the employer for details of the ballot result.

D.6.1.1.4   That the industrial action involves employees breaching their contracts of employment, or the commission of some other industrial tort.

D.6.1.2   For picketing injunctions:

D.6.1.2.1   A brief history of the facts leading to the dispute about which individuals are picketing.

D.6.1.2.2   The identity of those on the picket line (where possible), including whether any picket is a union official (whether paid or unpaid).

D.6.1.2.3   The activities of those on the picket line.

D.6.1.3   For both types:

D6.1.3.1   That the employer will suffer serious damage as a result of the industrial action or picketing.

D.6.1.3.2   That there is a serious issue to be tried.

D.6.1.3.3   That damages would not be an adequate remedy, either because the potential loss is unquantifiable or because the damage suffered would be in excess of the relevant union's maximum damage limits (see D.4.2.2) or because the likely damage to the employer goes beyond the immediate loss of business.

D.6.1.3.4   That the balance of convenience is in favour of maintaining normal production, and preserving the status quo.

D.6.1.3.5   That, should an injunction be awarded and the employer undertake to compensate the union for any damage suffered by the union in the event that the injunction was wrongly granted in the first place, the employer can afford to pay any such damages.

D.6.2   The employer should seek to give the union or, if known, the union's normal solicitors, notice of the intention to apply *ex parte* for an injunction.

D.6.3   If the injunction is granted it should be endorsed with a penal notice, informing those upon whom it is served that any breach will be a contempt of court, and served personally upon all the defendants. If the injunction is ignored, the trade union itself or any of its officers who can be shown to have knowledge of the injunction but who have nevertheless ignored it may be committed for contempt of court.

D.6.4   The application for committal may be made by the employer upon motion to the court. If there has been a contempt, any individual found to be in contempt may be fined or imprisoned, and the union may be fined or its assets may be sequestrated until the union has purged its contempt. Sequestration will only be granted if disobedience to the original injunction has been deliberate.

E Dismissal

All employees have the right not to be unfairly or wrongfully dismissed. These rights are distinct but overlapping.

Wrongful dismissal

An employee is wrongfully dismissed if, without cause, he is dismissed without notice (unless his contract provides it may summarily be terminated upon payment of money in lieu of notice) or without money in lieu of notice. The notice period is that set out in the contract, by implication, or in accordance with the statutory minimum given the employee's length of service (see A.8).

An employer may legitimately terminate an employee's employment without notice or money in lieu of notice if the employee has committed gross misconduct or some other serious breach of his contract of employment such as dishonesty, disobedience or serious incompetence. The test whether an employee has committed a sufficiently serious breach of contract is similar to the test whether an employee's conduct or capability is such that he can be fairly dismissed (see E.6 to E.8).

If an employer, without legitimate reason, summarily terminates an employee's contract, the employee is entitled to money in lieu of notice. This is quantified by calculating the net payments which the employee would have received during the balance of his notice period. The first £30,000 of any termination payment is tax-free (sections 148 and 188, Income and Corporation Taxes Act 1988), and any balance above £30,000 is grossed up at the employee's marginal tax rate to arrive at the final figure (see E.13.3).

In addition, if procedural requirements such as disciplinary and warning procedures are incorporated into contracts of employment, but are ignored, this could give rise to a claim by the employee for damages representing the salary he would have received had proper warning procedures been undertaken, up to the date when the employer could lawfully have terminated the contract.

Because the right to damages for wrongful dismissal is a common law right rather than a statutory right, the limitations and restrictions imposed by statute do not apply. For example, there is no minimum service requirement before one can claim damages for wrongful dismissal. In addition, an employee is not entitled to damages for wrongful dismissal merely because an employer has not followed fair procedural requirements, or because any serious breach by the employee of the contract of employment was not given as the reason for dismissal but was discovered, say, subsequent to dismissal.

Damages for wrongful dismissal and unfair dismissal to some extent overlap. An element of the compensation payment for unfair dismissal will be money in lieu of notice. Therefore, it will generally only be in employees' interests to sue for damages for wrongful dismissal instead of or as well as for compensation for unfair dismissal if the employee is a high earner and/or has a substantial notice period, or if the employee does not have the relevant length of service to qualify for compensation for unfair dismissal.

Unfair dismissal

In addition, most employees are entitled to claim compensation for unfair dismissal. An employee has to overcome certain hurdles. The most important hurdle is that, in order to be entitled to compensation for unfair dismissal, an employee must have worked 16 hours or more a week, continuously, for two years or more, or 8 hours or more a week, continuously, for five years or more. The only exceptions to this general rule are if the employee is dismissed because he is or is not a member of a particular union or has participated in union affairs at an appropriate time, or is dismissed as a result of race or sex discrimination, in which case there is no minimum time limit.

Grounds for dismissal

In respect of all qualifying employees, an employer must show that the reason for dismissal is a statutorily fair reason. The reasons are set out in section 57, EPCA 1978 and relate to incapability, lack of qualifications, misconduct, redundancy or breach of statutory provisions. There is also a catch-all ground of 'some other substantial reason which would justify dismissal'. It is automatically fair to dismiss someone to safeguard national security, or to dismiss someone while they are taking part in an official strike or industrial action when all those in a similar position are dismissed, or while taking part in unofficial action (see D.4.1.3 and D.4.1.4). It is automatically unfair to dismiss an employee on the basis of convictions which are spent under the Rehabilitation of Offenders Act 1974, a woman because she is pregnant or for a reason connected with pregnancy, reasons connected with membership or non-membership of or participation in the activities of an independent trade union or for a reason connected with a transfer of undertaking.

Although generally an employee is dismissed by the employer's direct act of termination, there are times when the employer's own actions are sufficiently in breach of a contract of employment as to justify the employee resigning and claiming constructive dismissal. This can only happen if the employer is in fundamental breach of the contract of employment, for example by reducing the employee's salary or status, or by treating him extremely high-handedly. Although it may be possible for an employer to argue that there is a legitimate reason for dismissing an employee who has been constructively dismissed, it is normally very difficult for the employer to succeed in such a claim.

Procedure

Even if the employer believes he has valid grounds for fairly dismissing an employee, he must still get the procedure right. In essence, he must make a detailed investigation, put the relevant facts before the employee, and invite the employee to put forward any explanation or evidence in mitigation which he feels may help his position. It is important that the procedures are followed. If they are not, an industrial tribunal will almost inevitably find that any dismissal is unfair unless the employer can show that he knew at the time of the dismissal that further investigation or a disciplinary meeting with the employee could never have made any difference. The exception will apply very rarely. However, even if there are procedural defects, while the dismissal may technically be unfair, if apart from technicalities it would have been fair, the employer may often successfully argue that any compensation payment should be substantially reduced, on occasion to nil.

Remedies

An employee who has been unfairly dismissed can claim reinstatement, re-engagement or compensation. Reinstatement and re-engagement mean, in effect, that the employee resumes his old position, or a similar position, on the same terms and conditions as before and is treated as though he had never been dismissed. In other words, the employee will receive back pay for the period from dismissal to the date of reinstatement or re-engagement. A court will generally only make a reinstatement or re-engagement order if satisfied that it is practicable for the employer to make available a suitable job, and that the relationship of trust and confidence between employer and employee is intact. It is rare that both these elements will come together, and it is therefore rare that reinstatement or re-engagement orders are made. If an order is made and the employer refuses to comply, the employee is entitled to compensation plus an additional costs penalty of between 26 and 52 weeks' pay, the week's pay being subject to the statutory maximum (£205 in respect of dismissals occurring after 1 April 1992).

The more normal remedy is compensation. This comes in two sections, the basic award, which is the equivalent of the statutory redundancy payment, and which is calculated by reference to age and length of service; and the compensatory award which seeks to quantify the actual loss suffered by the employee. This award is, however, subject to a statutory maximum of £10,000 which means that it rarely provides a complete remedy for employees earning substantial salaries. The compensatory award can be reduced if the employee is found to have contributed to some extent to his own dismissal.

In addition, employees subject to long notice periods or earning substantial salaries would be wise to bring proceedings against the employer for wrongful dismissal in the High Court or county court, which would entitle them to additional damages in the event that the £10,000 statutory maximum will be insufficient to compensate them.

Court procedure

Employees must make a complaint of unfair dismissal to the industrial tribunal within three months of the date of dismissal. If the employee fails to do so, he will not succeed in his claim. On the other hand, an employee has six years from the date of dismissal within which to bring a claim in the High Court or county court for damages for wrongful dismissal.

E.1   UNFAIR DISMISSAL — GENERAL CHECKLIST

E.1.1   Issues

E.1.1.1   The employee must prove that he has been dismissed, either directly by the employer or as a result of constructive dismissal (see E.4).

E.1.1.2   Is the employee in one of the categories which prevents him from bringing a claim for unfair dismissal (see E.3.1)?

E.1.1.3   Has the employee got the necessary continuity of service (see E.3.2)?

E.1.1.4   What is the reason for dismissal? Is it a fair reason (see E.5 to E.10)? If the employer has not made it clear why the employee is being dismissed, any employee continuously employed for two years or more should request written reasons for his dismissal (see E.5.5).

E.1.1.5   Has the employer followed the correct procedure (see E.7.3 (incompetence), E.8.1 and E.8.3 (ill health) and E.11 (misconduct/ some other substantial reason))?

E.1.1.6   Consider remedies. Does the employee want to be reinstated or re-engaged? Is this practicable? If not, what compensation/damages are due (see E.12 and E.13)?

E.1.2   **Factual issues to be covered**

E.1.2.1   Identity of employer, and any associated employer.

E.1.2.2   Length of service of employee.

E.1.2.3   Contractual terms — value of salary/wages and benefits, plus general contractual obligations and entitlements, for example duties, hours worked, etc. Documents should evidence contractual terms, for example letter of appointment, contract, amendment letters, staff handbook, collective agreement, etc. Custom and practice may, too, be relevant.

E.1.2.4   The reason for any termination of employment. Is the stated reason the true reason?

E.1.2.5   Does the employee retain any company property? If so, this should be returned.

E.1.2.6   What warnings were given earlier to the employee? What warning, consultation and disciplinary procedures were held relating to the dismissal?

E.1.2.7   What efforts had the employee made to find a new job? Has he retained details? He should. Has he properly mitigated his loss?

E.1.2.8   Is it practicable to reappoint the employee in his old or any similar job?

E.1.2.9   Has the employee received any settlement payment?

E.1.2.10   Are there any post-termination restrictive covenants in the contract? Do these apply? Is the employee breaking them, and if so will the court enforce them?

E.1.3   **General considerations**

E.1.3.1   *Costs*

E.1.3.1.1   Legal aid is not available for industrial tribunal claims (save for initial advice), though it is for appeals to the employment appeals tribunal (EAT) and for claims in the county court and High Court. An employee may obtain assistance from his trade union or the Free Representation Unit.

E.1.3.1.2   Normally, in the industrial tribunal and EAT, each party pays its own legal costs whatever the outcome, unless one party has been particularly vexatious or frivolous. In the High Court or county court, in the absence of any material payment into court, the unsuccessful party normally pays a proportion of the winner's legal costs.

E.1.3.2   *Timing*

Industrial tribunal proceedings normally come to court within three to nine months, High Court and county court proceedings normally come to court within six months to two years (depending upon their complexity).

E.1.3.3   *Evidence*

All facts relied upon must be proved, either by reference to documents or by oral witness evidence.

E.1.3.4   *Settlement negotiations*

If there is any prospect of settlement, it should be explored to save costs, management time, possible adverse publicity and uncertainty.

E.1.3.5   *Order of cases*

If proceedings for unfair and wrongful dismissal are brought, the parties should each consider which court they would wish to hear the application first. Employers generally prefer actions to be heard first in the High and county courts, and tribunals will normally award a stay of their proceedings pending the outcome of any wrongful dismissal case.

E.2   WRONGFUL DISMISSAL

E.2.1   Grounds for wrongful dismissal

E.2.1.1   where the employer without cause summarily terminates the employee's contract of employment (unless the contract provides it may summarily be terminated upon payment of money in lieu of notice); or

E.2.1.2   where the employer without cause dismisses the employee without money in lieu of notice. This may technically still be a breach of contract if there is no provision which allows the employer to terminate the contract of employment immediately upon payment in lieu of notice, though if a proper payment in lieu of notice is made, the employee will have suffered no damage.

E.2.1.3   Where the employer ignores contractual procedural requirements such as disciplinary and warning procedures which are expressly or impliedly incorporated into the employee's contract of employment, for example because expressly referred to in the contract, staff handbook or collective agreement.

E.2.2   The employer's defence

E.2.2.1   An employer can defeat a claim for damages for wrongful dismissal on the basis that the employee had previously committed material breach of contract. A breach of contract may be a breach of an express term of a contract or it may be that the employee has shown himself to be so incompetent or to have so misconducted himself as to entitle the employer to terminate the contract. In essence, the tests to be applied as to whether the employee's incompetence or misconduct are sufficiently serious to justify dismissal are the same as those which apply in unfair dismissal (see E.6 to E.8). The court will examine all the employee's conduct before dismissal, whether or not the employer knew of the conduct before he terminated the contract.

E.2.2.2   The employer may argue that he gave the employee proper notice of the termination of his contract of employment before the date of dismissal. An employee is not entitled both to work out his notice period and to have money in lieu of notice following the expiry of that notice period. For the appropriate length of an employee's notice period, see A.8.1.

E.2.3   Consequences

E.2.3.1   *Damages*

If an employee succeeds in demonstrating to the court that he has been wrongfully dismissed because his contract of employment was terminated without notice or without money in lieu of notice and there was no just cause for this, he will be entitled to recover damages. For calculation of damages, see E.13.3. In essence, the amount of damages will be the value of the employee's salary and benefits for the balance of the outstanding notice period. The employer may seek to reduce this sum in three ways:

E.2.3.1.1   *Mitigation of loss*

The employer will argue that the employee has a duty to mitigate his loss. This means that the employee must make all reasonable steps to find alternative employment. If he does so during the unexpired portion of the notice period, he must give credit to the employer for the sums he has received pursuant to his new employment as a result of his mitigation of loss.

E.2.3.1.2   *Discount for accelerated payment*

This is, in effect, reverse interest. If an employer pays an employee, upon termination of his employment without notice, money representing the salary the employee would have earned over the following, say, six months, the employer is entitled to reduce the total payment on the basis that the 'present value of the money' is actually greater than the aggregate of the salary payments over the six-month period: the rationale is that the employee could, if he so wished, place the money in a deposit account immediately and earn interest upon all the sums in his account even though in the normal course of events he would not have received all the salary payments immediately.

E.2.3.1.3   *Golden handshake payment*

Sections 148 and 188 of the Income and Corporation Taxes Act 1988 provide that the first £30,000 of any payment made in consideration of the termination of an employee's contract of employment, or in respect of loss of office, is tax-free. The employee is only entitled to be compensated for the actual loss suffered, and therefore to the extent that the loss is less than £30,000, the employer is entitled to deduct from the total payment the tax and national insurance contributions which the employee would otherwise have paid during the relevant notice period.

E.2.3.2   If an employer ignores contractual procedural requirements before implementing any dismissal, in addition to general damages the employee may be entitled to damages representing the salary he would have received had proper warning procedures been undertaken, up to the date when the employer could properly have terminated the contract having carried out the relevant procedures. Damages under this head will normally be in the region of two weeks' salary and benefits.

E.2.3.3   *Effect on post-termination provisions*

If the employer wrongly terminates the employee's contract of employment, then the contract ceases to be effective from that date and post-termination provisions such as restrictive covenants cease to have any effect.

E.2.4 Differences between wrongful and unfair dismissals

E.2.4.1 In relation to unfair dismissal, the employer must demonstrate to the industrial tribunal the actual reason for the dismissal, and must then show that this dismissal was fair. Breaches of contract on the employee's part after dismissal may only be relied upon to reduce the damages ultimately payable. However, for wrongful dismissal an employer will be able to rely upon any prior breach of contract by the employee to justify a summary dismissal, whether or not the employer knew of the breach at the date of dismissal.

E.2.4.2 If an employer fails to follow either contractual or general procedural requirements, any dismissal will generally be unfair. The only exception is when the employer can show that he knew at the time of the dismissal that procedural steps such as a disciplinary meeting could never have made any difference. On the other hand, save where contractual warning procedures have been totally ignored, when the position is as set out in E.2.3.2, an employer will not be penalised in any action for wrongful dismissal if he fails to follow fair procedural requirements.

E.2.4.3 An employer will be held to have unfairly dismissed an employee if he treated more leniently another employee who behaved in a similar fashion to the dismissed employee. For wrongful dismissal, the court will look only at whether the employee's conduct has been sufficiently serious to amount to a breach of contract which would justify dismissal. Precedent is immaterial, save that employees treated more leniently without reason may be cited by the employee as examples to illustrate that the conduct in question could not have been sufficiently serious to justify dismissal.

E.2.4.4 An employee who believes he has been unfairly dismissed must bring a complaint before the industrial tribunal within three months of the date of termination of employment. An employee who wishes to claim damages for wrongful dismissal must bring proceedings in a High Court or county court within six years of the date of termination of employment.

E.2.4.5 The amount of compensation for unfair dismissal to which an employee is entitled is limited by statute. There is no such limit in respect of damages for wrongful dismissal.

E.2.4.6 It is only in the very rarest circumstances — generally when the employer is a public authority or similar body with alternative departments in which the employee could be employed — that an employee will be 're-instated' in a wrongful dismissal claim. In relation to unfair dismissal, an employee can claim the remedies of re-instatement or re-engagement. However, even if the remedy is sought in such cases, it is not often granted.

E.3	**UNFAIR DISMISSAL — BASIC INFORMATION**
E.3.1	**Categories of employees who are not entitled to bring claims for unfair dismissal**
E.3.1.1	Those working 16 hours or more per week who have less than two years' continuous employment (see E.3.2)
E.3.1.2	Those working 8 hours or more but less than 16 hours per week who have less than five years' continuous employment (see E.3.2).
E.3.1.3	Those working less than 8 hours per week (see E.3.2).
E.3.1.4	Those employed under contracts for services such as freelance workers or independent contractors (see A.1).
E.3.1.5	Those working under illegal contracts, though if an employer persuades an employee to accept an illegal contract (for example, one which enables the employer to defraud the Inland Revenue) or if the employee does not realise that the contract is illegal when he enters into it, the employee will still be able to rely upon the contract.
E.3.1.6	Those above the normal retiring age for that category of employee employed by the particular employer, or those aged 65, whichever is the lower age limit in the particular case.
E.3.1.7	Those ordinarily working outside Great Britain at the time of their dismissal, either because they are obliged to do so under the terms of their contract, or, if the terms are inconclusive, because the employee's base is outside Great Britain.
E.3.1.8	Those engaged on a fixed-term contract of one year or more who have specifically agreed to exclude their right to claim unfair dismissal, and whose employment is terminated on the expiry of the fixed term.
E.3.1.9	Those in respect of whom an agreed settlement has been made through the intervention of ACAS.

E.3.1.10   Those not unambiguously dismissed and given a definite leaving date (unless the employee leaves in circumstances of constructive dismissal — see E.4.3).

E.3.1.11   Those whose contracts of employment are frustrated by some circumstance unforeseen when the contract was entered into which renders performance of the contract very different from what was originally contemplated — for example, because the employee is severely incapacitated for a very long time as a result of sickness or because the employee is imprisoned.

E.3.1.12   Those who resign, in the absence of any situation of constructive dismissal, unless they have been told by their employers to 'resign or be sacked', in which case the resignation will be treated as a dismissal.

E.3.1.13   Those employed in the police service.

E.3.1.14   Certain Crown employees, particularly those in the armed forces.

E.3.1.15   Share fishermen and people employed on board ships registered outside Great Britain. Note, those working on ships registered in Great Britain will be eligible to claim compensation for unfair dismissal unless they are wholly employed or resident outside Great Britain.

E.3.2   Continuous employment

E.3.2.1   In deciding the number of hours an employee works per week, first look at the contract of employment. If a subsisting contract normally involves employment for 16 hours or more per week (or, as the case may be, 8 hours or more per week), even if occasionally it involves a shorter working week or if occasionally the employee works less, for example through sickness, the employee will have passed the continuity hurdle.

E.3.2.2   If in any week an employee is not bound by contract to work at least 16 (or, as the case may be, 8 hours) per week, and does not do so, this breaks continuity and the employee will have to start again to build up two years' or five years' continuous service.

E.3.2.3   It is important to remember that the test is the number of hours of work per week provided for by the contract. It is not sufficient merely to aggregate the number of hours worked each week over the previous two-year or five-year period, and from that to deduce an average number of hours per week.

E.3.2.4   *Bridging rules*

The employee will still be counted as having continuous service, even though there is no subsisting contract of employment, where:

E.3.2.4.1   The employee is absent through sickness or injury for up to 26 consecutive weeks.

E.3.2.4.2   The employee is absent on account of a temporary cessation of work, for example as a result of a lay-off.

E.3.2.4.3   The absence is by arrangement or custom, where it is understood, before the absence begins, that the employee will be taken back following the absence, for example a secondment or sabbatical.

E.3.2.4.4   The employee is absent from work through pregnancy or maternity leave (provided the employee returns to work within the appropriate time limits) (see C.5).

E.3.2.4.5   The employee is absent as a result of having taken part in industrial action, though the number of weeks of industrial action is disregarded in deciding the total number of weeks the employee has worked.

E.3.2.4.6   An employee is reinstated or re-engaged following any dismissal, when the period when he was in fact not working for the employer is still regarded as part of his continuous service.

E.3.2.4.7   An employee's employer changes as a result of a transfer of undertaking, when the employee's employment with the new employer is deemed to have commenced on the date the employee started working for the old employer.

E.3.2.4.8   An employee's job is transferred from his employing company to that of an associated employer (i.e., a company of which the other, directly or indirectly, has control, or a company which is under the ultimate control of the same person who controls the original employer), when employment is deemed to have commenced on the date when the employee started working for the first employer.

E.3.2.4.9   A personal employer dies and his personal representatives maintain an employee's employment, when the employment will be deemed to have begun when the first employment began.

E.3.2.4.10   There is a change in the partners, personal representatives or trustees who employ an employee, when the employment will be deemed to have begun when the first employment began.

E.3.3 Start date when determining the period of continuous employment

The period starts on the date the employment commences, by virtue of the contract of employment, and not necessarily upon the date when the employee's duties began. For example, an employee who is told that his contract of employment will begin on Friday 1 January, but who does therefore not start work until Monday 4 January, will nevertheless be treated as though his employment started on 1 January.

E.3.4 Termination date

The termination date may be:

E.3.4.1 The date any notice period given expires (even if less than the notice period to which the employee is contractually or statutorily entitled).

E.3.4.2 The date a fixed-term contract comes to an end.

E.3.4.3 If payment is given in lieu of notice but dismissal takes effect immediately, the termination date is the date of dismissal.

E.3.4.4 If the employee is dismissed with notice, but is not required to work during the notice period, the termination date is the date of expiry of the notice period, even if the employee is immediately given money in lieu of working out the notice period.

E.3.4.5 The date on which the parties agree that the employment will terminate.

E.3.4.6 The date on which the employer terminates the employment agreement — though if the employee is given no notice or little notice the effective date of termination (EDT) will be the date of dismissal plus (unless the employee has agreed to short notice or money in lieu of notice) the period of statutory notice to which the employee would have been entitled. This EDT applies for all purposes save for the purpose of calculating the period within which any unfair dismissal or resignation complaint must be lodged, which must be three months from the date of actual dismissal rather than from the EDT.

E.3.4.7 If summary dismissal is communicated by letter, the date of termination is the date when the employee read the letter or first had the opportunity to read the letter, which is normally later than the date upon which the letter was sent.

E.3.4.8   If the employer serves notice on the employee to terminate a contract and the employee subsequently serves a counter notice terminating the contract on an earlier date, the termination date is nevertheless the date when the employer's notice would have expired.

E.3.4.9   If an employee resigns and claims constructive dismissal, the EDT is the date of resignation plus the period of statutory notice to which the employee would have been entitled. (For effect of EDT, see E.3.4.6.)

E.3.4.10   If an employee is told to resign or be dismissed, the EDT is the date the resignation takes effect plus the period of statutory notice to which the employee is entitled. (For effect of EDT, see E.3.4.6.)

               Note: Any appeal in any disciplinary procedure following dismissal is to be ignored for the purposes of estimating the termination date.

E.4   DISMISSAL

E.4.1   Direct dismissal

E.4.1.1   Words of dismissal, whether oral or written, should be unequivocal and should set a date for the termination of employment.

E.4.1.2   Words spoken in the heat of the moment (for example, 'get out and never come back' said at the end of a fierce argument) generally do not amount to a dismissal unless they are repeated subsequently. An employer should allow an employee apparently resigning in such circumstances a couple of days to cool off and reconsider.

E.4.2   Expiry of a fixed-term contract

               If a fixed-term contract expires and is not renewed, this will be a dismissal.

E.4.3   Constructive dismissal

E.4.3.1   Constructive dismissal occurs when an employer's conduct — actual or threatened — is a serious breach of the employment contract and the employee elects to treat that breach as 'repudiatory' and resigns as a result.

E.4.3.2   The employer's breach of contract must be sufficiently important to justify the employee resigning, or must be the last in a series of less important incidents.

E.4.3.3   The employer's conduct must amount to a fundamental breach of contract. Unreasonable behaviour not amounting to a breach, for example a refusal to allow compassionate leave, is not sufficient. The employer's actions will not amount to a constructive dismissal, however unreasonable, if there is an express contractual term allowing him to take that action. For example, a provision in a contract, or in a collective agreement or staff handbook if their terms are incorporated into the contract of employment, that an employer is entitled to vary shift patterns, will enable the employer to do so. However, the employer has a duty not to conduct himself in a manner, without reasonable or proper cause, likely to destroy or seriously damage the relationship of trust and confidence between the parties. Thus any change in shift pattern could not be wholly unreasonable, and might require reasonable prior notice.

E.4.3.4   An employee must leave in response to the breach and not for some other reason. In any resignation letter an employee would be wise to set out the employer's breach on which he relies to resign and claim constructive dismissal.

E.4.3.5   An employee must act promptly in resigning following the breach or he may be deemed to have waived the breach and agreed to vary the contract. What is 'prompt' will vary according to circumstances, but will normally be within at least one or two months.

E.4.3.6   The employee may rely upon the conduct of anyone employed by the employer in a supervisory capacity, and not only upon the conduct of the particular person who has the power to dismiss the employee.

E.4.3.7   The following are examples of events of constructive dismissal:

E.4.3.7.1   Reduction in pay.

E.4.3.7.2   Removal of contractual benefits.

E.4.3.7.3   Change in hours.

E.4.3.7.4   Change in shift pattern in the absence of an express contractual provision allowing the change.

E.4.3.7.5   Requiring an employee to move location to somewhere beyond the reasonable daily reach of his home, in the absence of an express contractual provision allowing mobility.

E.4.3.7.6   Requiring an employee to transfer location of work without reasonable notice.

E.4.3.7.7   Significantly varying the employee's duties, for example removing one particularly enjoyable aspect of an employee's job specification if this reduces job satisfaction or lowers prestige.

E.4.3.7.8   Lowering an employee's status.

E.4.3.7.9   Sexual harassment by any other employee.

E.4.3.7.10   Failure on the part of management to investigate allegations of sexual harassment.

E.4.3.7.11   Imposing a disciplinary suspension without pay, unless the employer is allowed to do so in the relevant disciplinary procedures.

E.4.3.7.12   Imposing a disciplinary punishment out of all proportion to the offence.

E.4.3.7.13   Laying off employees without pay, in the absence of an express contractual provision allowing the employer to do so.

E.4.3.7.14   Capricious or arbitrary singling out of an individual or group of individuals for inferior treatment, for example not awarding one employee a pay rise awarded to other employees, for no reason.

E.4.3.7.15   Accusing an employee, without any foundation, of inability to perform his job.

E.4.3.7.16   Failing to give an employee the necessary support to perform his functions and duties properly.

E.4.3.7.17   Humiliating employees, for example by reprimanding them derisively in front of their colleagues.

E.4.3.7.18   Failing to provide a satisfactory working environment to enable employees to work, for example consistently failing to supply appropriate tools.

E.4.3.7.19   Requiring employees to work in unsafe conditions.

E.4.3.7.20   Refusing to provide work for an employee if the employee's job is such that his skills constantly need exercising, such as scientists and doctors.

E.4.3.7.21   Refusing to provide work where a significant proportion of the employee's remuneration is based upon commission.

E.4.3.7.22   Failing to treat an employee with dignity.

E.4.3.8   The following conduct does *not* amount to an event of constructive dismissal:

E.4.3.8.1   Minor alterations to the employee's contractual terms.

E.4.3.8.2   Changes allowed by the contract of employment.

E.4.3.8.3   A delay in payment of wages, if not substantial.

E.4.3.8.4   Lack of consultation over the appointment of a subordinate.

E.4.3.8.5   An occasion where the employer genuinely believes, albeit erroneously, that he is entitled by his contract to act in the manner he has.

E.5   **REASON FOR DISMISSAL**

In any dismissal action, the burden is on the employer to show the reason for dismissal. In a case of wrongful dismissal, the employer must then show that the reason is sufficiently serious to have justified the employer terminating the contract, whether he knew of the reason at the date of termination or otherwise. For unfair dismissal, the employer must show what the reason for dismissal was, that it was the actual reason why the decision to dismiss was taken, and that it was a fair reason.

E.5.1   **Potentially fair reasons**

These are set out in section 57, EPCA 1978 and are:

E.5.1.1   That the employee was incapable (measured by reference to skills, aptitude, health or any physical or mental quality) of performing the work of the kind he was currently employed by the employer to do (see E.7).

E.5.1.2   That the employee lacked the qualifications required to perform work of the kind that he was currently employed by the employer to do.

E.5.1.3   Misconduct (see E.6).

E.5.1.4   Redundancy (see Chapter F).

E.5.1.5   That if the employee were to continue to be employed in the position he held, either he or the employer would be in breach of some statutory provision (see E.10.1).

E.5.1.6   Some other substantial reason which will justify dismissal (see E.10.2).

E.5.2   Automatically fair reasons

E.5.2.1   The dismissal of an employee to safeguard national security. This applies whether or not the employee is a civil servant or member of the armed forces. He may, for example, be an employee of a defence contractor.

E.5.2.2   Dismissal of an employee while he is taking part in an official strike or industrial action when all those taking similar action are also dismissed, or of any employee taking part in unofficial strike action (see D.4.1.2 and D.4.1.3).

E.5.3   Automatically unfair reasons

E.5.3.1   Dismissal of a woman because she is pregnant or for a reason connected with pregnancy (see C.3).

E.5.3.2   Dismissal of an employee for reasons connected with membership or non-membership of, or participation in, the activities of an independent trade union. Note, in this instance an employee is entitled to an additional special award of damages, and may also bring a claim against the employer whatever the period of his continuous employment (see E.9).

E.5.3.3   Dismissal of an employee because of a reason connected with a transfer of an undertaking (see G.4.3).

E.5.3.4   Dismissal of an employee on the basis of criminal convictions which are deemed to have been spent under the Rehabilitation of Offenders Act 1974.

E.5.3.5   It is proposed that dismissal of an employee for questioning the adequacy of health and safety procedures will be unfair. (See Appendix.)

E.5.4   Time for assessing the reason for dismissal in unfair dismissal cases

E.5.4.1   A dismissal must be fair based upon the facts known to the employer either at the date the employee was given notice of his dismissal, or, if there is an appeal, at the date of the announcement of the appeal decision.

E.5.4.2   An industrial tribunal cannot substitute its own reasoning and opinions for those of the employer. The matter must be judged by the objective standard of the way in which a reasonable employer in that line of business of that size in those circumstances would have behaved. The tribunal must ask the question: 'Was dismissal, as a sanction, one within the range of reasonable responses to the conduct which a reasonable employer might reasonably have imposed?' It is irrelevant whether other employers might have behaved more leniently towards the individual.

E.5.4.3   Subsequently discovered conduct. While conduct discovered after notice of dismissal or announcement of any appeal cannot be used to justify the dismissal in any unfair dismissal proceedings, it may be taken into account in the following circumstances:

E.5.4.3.1   It may be relied upon to show the employer was reasonable in reaching any decision he did, before dismissal, about the employee's performance or conduct.

E.5.4.3.2   It may affect remedies. If subsequently discovered conduct is very serious, it could lead to a finding that it was not just and equitable for the tribunal to make any compensatory award at all.

E.5.4.3.3   If new facts arise between the notice of dismissal and the termination date which show that the employer's conduct was unwarranted, this can be relied upon by the employee to show that the ultimate dismissal was unfair. For example, if an employer gives an employee notice of termination of his employment as a result of misconduct but, before the termination date, discovers that it was another employee who committed the acts of misconduct in question, if the employer still upholds the original employee's dismissal, this will be unfair.

E.5.4.3.4   An employer can rely upon information relating to the original reason for dismissal received during the course of any appeal procedure, though he may not use such information to introduce a fresh reason for dismissal. In those circumstances, if the employer wishes to rely upon the new information as a reason for dismissal, the original dismissal should be revoked upon appeal and further dismissal proceedings instituted.

E.5.4.3.5   It may be relied upon to justify a wrongful dismissal.

E.5.4.4   The employer must show he has acted reasonably in all the circumstances in treating the reason for dismissal as a sufficiently serious one to dismiss the employee.

E.5.5   **Written reasons for dismissal**

E.5.5.1   Employees who have been continuously employed for two years or more have the right to request written reasons for their dismissal. An employer should respond to such requests within 14 days. (See Appendix.)

E.5.5.2   If the employer refuses to give reasons, he is liable to pay the employee two weeks' pay.

E.5.5.3   An industrial tribunal is not bound to accept the employer's stated reasons for dismissal if it finds that the reasons given conceal the true reason, but in any tribunal proceedings the employer is bound by the facts given in support of any dismissal, though not necessarily by the legal label given to those facts. When considering the reasons the tribunal will seek to ensure that they are genuinely held by the employer.

E.6   **MISCONDUCT**

E.6.1   **Disciplinary code**

E.6.1.1   A disciplinary code may be expressly incorporated into an employee's contract of employment. If it is, its provisions should be adhered to. In the absence of an express disciplinary code, any industrial tribunal will have regard to the ACAS disciplinary code. It will also expect any contractual disciplinary code to be along similar lines.

E.6.1.2   The ACAS Code of Practice provides that facts should be established promptly following any disciplinary matter and an individual should be interviewed and given the opportunity to state his or her case and be advised of any rights under the procedure before a decision is made.

E.6.1.3   *Minor offences.* The Code states that in the case of minor offences the individual should be given a formal oral warning or, if the issue is more serious, a written warning setting out the nature of the offence and the likely consequence of further offences. Further misconduct might warrant a final written warning, which should contain a statement that any occurrence would lead to suspension or dismissal. A further offence could result in dismissal. Minor offences include lateness, taking too long meal breaks, minor acts of insubordination or rudeness and so on.

E.6.1.4   *Gross misconduct.* Any single act of gross misconduct (ie serious breach of contract) will be sufficient to justify immediate dismissal without notice, money in lieu of notice or compensation.

E.6.1.5   Misconduct involves some deliberate or reckless act or omission. Negligence or carelessness will generally be regarded as incapability (see E.7).

E.6.2   Refusal to obey a lawful order

E.6.2.1   Refusal to obey a lawful order is misconduct. The nature of the refusal and the importance of the order will determine whether the misconduct is minor or gross. To determine what is lawful, one must look at the contract and any other incorporated documents such as a collective agreement or staff handbook, and at custom and practice.

E.6.2.2   Examples of misconduct include:

E.6.2.2.1   Refusal to comply with safety requirements.

E.6.2.2.2   Refusal to move location if the contract provides that the employee can be required to move to a proposed new site.

E.6.2.2.3   Refusal to perform a task which the employee is contractually obliged to perform.

E.6.2.2.4   Refusal to work reasonable overtime if the contract provides that the employees must work overtime. (*Note*: following the UK's expected implementation of the proposed EC working time directive, it would not be reasonable to expect an employee to work more than 48 hours per week in total.)

E.6.2.3   The following acts would not amount to misconduct under this head:

E.6.2.3.1   Refusal by employees to work in dangerous conditions.

E.6.2.3.2   Refusal to obey an unlawful order, for example to falsify accounts.

E.6.2.3.3   Refusal to work overtime if the employee is not contractually obliged to do so.

E.6.2.4   Refusal to accept change in terms and conditions of employment, if those changes are justifiable because of pressing business need on the part of the employer, will not amount to misconduct on the part of the employee but may amount to some other substantial reason which would justify the employer dismissing the employee (see A.6).

E.6.3   **Breaches of discipline**

E.6.3.1   If the employer's disciplinary code sets out an exhaustive list of disciplinary offences, no additional offences omitted from the list may be relied upon. If the disciplinary code sets out examples only of breaches of disciplinary procedure, then items which are not set out in the list may nevertheless, if sufficiently serious, be categorised by the employer as misconduct.

E.6.3.2   Examples of breaches of discipline are:

E.6.3.2.1   Drunkenness at work.

E.6.3.2.2   Being unfit to work as a result of drug abuse.

E.6.3.2.3   Theft of employer's, colleagues', clients' or suppliers' property.

E.6.3.2.4   Physical violence or fighting.

E.6.3.2.5   Threatening behaviour.

E.6.3.2.6   Bad language.

E.6.3.2.7   Rudeness.

E.6.3.2.8   Fraud, for example falsifying timesheets, or giving false information on a curriculum vitae (for example, not disclosing a past, unspent conviction).

E.6.3.2.9   Gross insubordination.

E.6.3.2.10   Working for or assisting a competitor or preparing to compete against the employer in future (though merely seeking alternative employment following the termination of the present contract is not unlawful).

E.6.3.2.11   Misusing or unlawfully disclosing confidential information.

E.6.3.2.12   Unauthorised use of or tampering with a computer.

E.6.3.2.13   Taking industrial action.

E.6.3.2.14   Taking bribes or secret commissions.

E.6.3.2.15   Serious breach of codes of relevant professional or governing bodies.

E.6.4   Criminal offences

E.6.4.1   Criminal offences should only merit dismissal if they relate in some way to the employee's duties, for example because they show that the employee is unsuitable for performing that type of work, or the offence renders the employee unacceptable to other employees.

E.6.4.2   Examples of criminal offences which justify dismissal:

E.6.4.2.1   Dishonesty (fraud, theft, etc.). This will normally justify dismissal unless, for example, the employee has been actively employed (i.e. not just on suspension) for a period after his conviction.

E.6.4.2.2   Sexual offences. These will justify dismissal if the employee's duties often put him in contact with women or children, especially vulnerable ones, for example where the job is involved in education or health.

E.6.4.3   Examples of criminal offences which do not justify dismissal:

E.6.4.3.1   Minor drugs or traffic offences. These will not usually justify dismissal unless, for example, drug addiction affects the employee's capability or the employee's job requires a clean driving licence.

E.7   INCOMPETENCE

E.7.1   If the employer honestly believes, on reasonable grounds, that the employee is incompetent, he may dismiss him. It is, however, very rare that an employer may fairly dismiss an employee for incompetence if the employee has not had proper appraisal and warning before a final decision is taken.

E.7.2   *Evidence of incompetence*

                The industrial tribunal must rely to a large extent on the evidence of the employee's superiors in deciding whether or not an employee has been incompetent. An employer should have specific examples of incompetence, for example:

E.7.2.1   Failure by the employee to perform part of his duties.

E.7.2.2   Complaints by colleagues or customers about the actions of the employee.

E.7.2.3   Inaccuracies committed by the employee.

E.7.2.4   Delays in finishing work by the employee.

E.7.2.5   Inflexibility and lack of adaptability on the part of the employee.

E.7.2.6   Slovenliness or persistent carelessness on the part of the employee.

Separate and dissimilar acts of incompetence may cumulatively be relied upon by the employer. The employee is to be judged by the standards to be expected of someone in his present job, even if he has been over-promoted by the employer: an employee cannot demand to be returned to his former position, though in these circumstances a prudent employer would seek to establish whether there are any lower-grade jobs to which the employee could be transferred.

E.7.3   Before dismissing an employee for incompetence, the employer will normally need to adopt the following *procedure*:

E.7.3.1   *Appraisal.* The employer should discuss with the employee the criticisms he has of the employee's performance. The employer should maintain a system to monitor the employee's progress.

E.7.3.2   *Warning.* The employer should warn the employee of the consequences of a failure to improve. This should, preferably, be in writing. The warning should set out:

E.7.3.2.1   Where the employee has failed to meet the required standards.

E.7.3.2.2   The time within which the employee must improve.

E.7.3.2.3   The fact that if the employee fails to improve, a further warning will be necessary (or, after the second warning, dismissal may be invoked).

E.7.3.3   *Opportunity to improve.* The employer must give the employee a reasonable period within which to improve. In establishing what is reasonable one must bear in mind the nature of the job, the employee's length of service, status and past performance. The employer should give the employee the necessary support and assistance to allow the employee to improve.

E.7.3.4   Employees of previously good standing and long service will require special attention by the employer before any dismissal is made. They should be given reasonably substantial periods within which to improve unless there are very obvious reasons why an employee has suddenly become incapable, for example:

E.7.3.4.1   The employee's capacity to do the job is altered, for example because of ill health.

E.7.3.4.2   The employee's job functions have altered, for example as a result of new technology.

E.7.3.4.3   The employee has failed to heed warnings.

E.7.4   Warnings for incompetence are not necessary in the following circumstances:

E.7.4.1   Gross incompetence or unsuitability.

E.7.4.2   Incompetence which has had serious physical consequences, for example where a pilot has incompetently landed a plane causing actual or potential injury to passengers and/or expensive equipment.

E.7.4.3   Incompetence which has serious economic consequences, for example deliberate or reckless incompetence leading to a loss of a whole production batch.

E.7.4.4   Incompetence where the employer reasonably believes that a warning would make no difference, for example where an employee refuses to admit that there is any need for him to improve.

E.7.4.5   An incompetent senior employee, who should appreciate what standards are required of him and whether he matches up to those standards. The employee must, however, be in a position to know (whether from his own experience or because he has been told his work is unsatisfactory) that he may be dismissed unless his work meets the required standards.

E.7.5   If an employer has dismissed the employee for incapability, care should be taken in drafting any reference so that the reference does not indicate that the employee was a perfectly satisfactory worker (for references, see A.8.3).

E.8   **ILL HEALTH**

Before dismissing an employee on the grounds of ill health, the employer should make proper enquiry into the actual state of the employee's health, its likely duration, and its effect upon the employee's ability to perform his tasks.

E.8.1   **Absenteeism**

E.8.1.1   Where the employee takes frequent short-term self-certificated absences, the employer should:

E.8.1.1.1   Review the employee's attendance record and the reasons given for it.

E.8.1.1.2   Give the employee the opportunity to explain his attendance record.

E.8.1.1.3   If the employee does not give a satisfactory explanation, he should be asked to see a doctor to consider whether medical treatment is necessary. Any genuine illness must be treated with sympathy and under normal illness procedures (see E.8.3).

E.8.1.1.4   If there is still no satisfactory explanation for the absences, the employee should be given a warning that further unwarranted absences are likely to result in dismissal.

E.8.1.1.5   The employer should interview the applicant after any subsequent absence to ascertain its cause.

E.8.1.1.6   If there is no improvement in the attendance record, and still no valid reason for the absences, the employer may dismiss the employee.

E.8.2   **Disability**

E.8.2.1   Where the employer knew, when he engaged the employee, of the existence and extent of a disability, he is most unlikely to be able fairly to dismiss the employee by reason only of the disability. In those circumstances the standard of work required of the employee will be that of a disabled person to do the particular job in hand.

E.8.2.2   Where an employee becomes disabled during the course of his employment, he should be treated in the same manner as employees suffering from other illnesses (see E.8.3).

E.8.3   Illness

E.8.3.1   Before taking any action regarding an employee's illness the employer should take the following steps:

E.8.3.1.1   Obtain a medical opinion. This medical opinion should be more detailed than a mere expression of opinion that an employee is unfit to work, unless the employee refuses to undergo a medical check up. An employee cannot be compelled (in the absence of an express contractual term) to undergo medical examinations.

E.8.3.1.2   Examine the sickness record.

E.8.3.1.3   Discuss the position with the employee and ask the employee for his own views on his health and abilities.

E.8.3.2   Having formed a reasoned opinion of the employee's medical state, the employer should consider the following factors:

E.8.3.2.1   The nature of the illness.

E.8.3.2.2   The likelihood of it recurring.

E.8.3.2.3   The length of absences likely and the intervening spaces of good health.

E.8.3.2.4   Whether the employee's tasks can smoothly be done by colleagues while the employee is absent.

E.8.3.2.5   The impact on colleagues of the employee's absence.

E.8.3.2.6   The employee's length of service.

E.8.3.2.7   The need for the employer to have employees of this nature in rude health (for example, deep-sea divers, heavy manual workers).

E.8.3.2.8   Whether the ill health might cause potential problems at the work place (for example, an epileptic may be thought not to be able to work with dangerous machinery).

E.8.3.2.9   Alternative employment (for example a desk job) for the employee. The employer is not however expected to create a special job for the employee but only to look to see whether he has any suitable vacancies.

E.8.3.2.10   The employer's sick pay scheme. Employers should generally not dismiss an employee who is still entitled to benefits under the scheme.

E.8.3.3   If it is clear that the employee will not within a reasonable time be able to resume his duties satisfactorily, and there are no alternative available jobs which the employee could be offered, it may be reasonable for the employer to dismiss the employee.

E.8.3.4   Very serious ill health, which will either mean the employee cannot in future carry out his old role or will be absent for long periods of time (at least more than the period when the employer's sick pay scheme operates) can mean that the contract terminates by frustration, and there is therefore no dismissal.

E.8.3.5   *AIDS*

An employer will generally not be able to dimiss an employee who is HIV positive unless AIDS has manifested itself and prevents the employee from working properly. The employer must consider the issues set out in E.8.3.2 in the normal way. The employer should seek to allay unreasoned fears of any of the employee's colleagues.

E.9   DISMISSAL FOR TRADE UNION MEMBERSHIP OR ACTIVITIES

E.9.1   Automatically unfair grounds

E.9.1.1   Dismissal of an employee because he is or is not a member of any or any particular trade union is automatically unfair. There can be no closed shop, and in general no policy whereby the employer refuses to employ union members.

E.9.1.2   It is automatically unfair to dismiss an employee because he has taken part in trade union activities involving his current employer at an appropriate time (i.e., outside working hours or within working hours with the employer's consent).

E.9.2   Examples of legitimate trade union activity for which it would be automatically unfair to dismiss an employee are:

E.9.2.1   An employee recruiting other employees to the union during a meal break.

E.9.2.2   A shop steward fairly representing the union's and the employer's position to his members during the course of a dispute.

E.9.3   Dismissal of union representatives who have undertaken the following activities has been held not to be automatically unfair:

E.9.3.1   The dismissal of a union member for constantly complaining about health and safety issues when he was not the health and safety representative or a union official.

E.9.3.2   The dismissal of a person acting in defiance of union policies.

E.9.3.3   The dismissal of a person who, while doing something which would normally be part of his union duties (for example, organising a strike ballot) does so maliciously or dishonestly (for example, by giving members false information about the issues in dispute).

E.9.4   General points

E.9.4.1   There is no minimum period of employment for the employee before he can bring a claim of unfair dismissal under these heads.

E.9.4.2   It is most unlikely that an employer will ever admit that the reason for dismissal could possibly be connected with union matters, but it will be for an industrial tribunal to examine whether the reason for dismissal given by the employer is the correct one, or whether the employee has established that the real reason was connected with his trade union activities.

E.9.4.3   An employee who succeeds in a claim that he has been unfairly dismissed for trade union reasons is entitled to additional compensation (see E.9.5).

E.9.5   Remedy

An employee unfairly dismissed because of trade union reasons is entitled to the following:

E.9.5.1   Basic award, calculated in accordance with F.9 but subject to a statutory minimum of £2,700.

E.9.5.2   Compensatory award, calculated in accordance with normal rules (see E.13.2).

E.9.5.3   If an employee seeks reinstatement or re-engagement, whether or not ordered, the employee will be entitled to a special award of *either* 104 × a week's pay (with no limit on the amount of a week's pay) but subject to a maximum of £26,800, *or* alternatively £13,400, whichever is greater in the specific case.

E.9.5.4   If an industrial tribunal makes a reinstatement order but the employer does not comply with it, the employee's special award is *either* 156 × a week's pay (with no limit on the amount of a week's pay) *or* alternatively £20,100, whichever is greater in the specific case.

E.9.5.5   The special award may be reduced if the tribunal believes it is just and equitable in all the circumstances so to do.

E.9.6   Application for interim relief

E.9.6.1   A person who believes he has been dismissed for trade union reasons may apply to an industrial tribunal for interim relief. The application must be presented to an industrial tribunal within seven days of the effective date of termination of employment (EDT).

E.9.6.2   An authorised official of the employee's trade union must within seven days of the EDT present a certificate to the tribunal stating that the employee is, or proposed to become, a member of the trade union, and there appear to be reasonable grounds for supposing that the principal reason for the dismissal was the one alleged in the employee's complaint.

E.9.6.3   An industrial tribunal must decide, before making an order for interim relief, that the employee has a 'pretty good chance' of succeeding in his claim that he has been dismissed for taking part in trade union activities or for his membership or non-membership of a trade union.

E.9.6.4   If the employee's claim succeeds, the employer will be asked to reinstate or re-engage the employee. If the employer refuses, or if he offers to re-engage but the employee reasonably refuses the offer, the industrial tribunal will in effect order that the employee be suspended on full pay until the hearing.

E.10   OTHER REASONS FOR DISMISSAL

E.10.1   Illegality

If an employer is to dismiss an employee under this head the employment must genuinely be in breach of the law. If the employer erroneously believes it does, then the dismissal may be fair for some other substantial reason but not under the heading of illegality. Examples of illegality include:

E.10.1.1   The employee losing a work permit.

E.10.1.2   The employee being disqualified from driving if driving is an essential part of the job.

E.10.1.3   The employee no longer having relevant professional qualifications (for example, an employed solicitor or doctor who is struck off the professional register).

Before dismissing on the ground of illegality the employer should consider whether he has any alternative vacancies which he could offer the employee that the employee would not legally be disqualified from performing. The employer does not have to create a suitable position if none is availble.

E.10.2   Some other substantial reason

E.10.2.1   Examples include:

E.10.2.1.1   An unreasonable refusal by the employee to accept changes in the terms and conditions of his employment whose imposition is necessary for pressing business reasons (see A.6).

E.10.2.1.2   The sexual orientation of the employee if it affects his job.

E.10.2.1.3   The employee's sexual conduct if it affects his ability to carry out his job. For example, it may be legitimate to dismiss an unmarried but pregnant school matron on the ground that her pregnancy sets a bad example to pupils, though it would not be fair to dismiss someone working in an office for having an affair with a colleague unless the affair had a serious detrimental effect upon work standards or other colleagues.

E.10.2.1.4   A personality clash if it disrupts the work place. An employer should first try to establish whether the position is remediable, for example by moving one of the employees to another department.

E.10.2.1.5   The dismissal of an employee at the request of a third party. The employer must take into account, however, the potential injustice to the employee before acting on the third party's request. This will only be a fair dismissal in exceptional cases, for example if a valued customer requires the employer to dismiss the employee, but it does not avail any employer who, for example, gives in to union pressure to dismiss an employee.

E.10.2.1.6   A breakdown of trust and confidence between employer and employee.

E.10.2.1.7   Imprisonment of an employee.

E.10.2.1.8   The wish of an employer to appoint his child to do the relevant job.

E.10.2.1.9   The protection of the employer's business, for example, where the employee refuses to sign a reasonable restrictive covenant.

E.10.2.1.10   A dismissal arising following a transfer of undertakings for an economic, technical or organisational reason entailing changes in the workforce (see G.4.3.2).

E.10.2.2   The following have been held not to justify dismissal:

E.10.2.2.1   A rumour that an employee would leave to start up a rival business.

E.10.2.2.2   The fact that a relation of the employee has been convicted of dishonesty.

E.10.2.2.3   The fact that an employee is looking for alternative employment.

E.10.2.3   No employee should be dismissed for some other substantial reason unless appropriate warning and consultation procedures are first carried out (see E.11).

E.10.3   Unfair selection for redundancy (see F.2, F.5, F.6 and F.7).

E.10.4   Reasons connected with transfers of undertaking (see G.4.3).

E.10.5   Reasons connected with pregnancy (see C.3).

E.11   PROCEDURE

Tribunals now lay great emphasis upon an employer following a fair procedure before warning or dismissing an employee. Though it is not true that any procedural irregularity renders a dismissal unfair, it is one of the factors that is taken into account when deciding whether an employer has acted reasonably in dismissing an employee. Tribunals will expect a procedure to be implemented unless the employer *knows* at the time he decides not to have any disciplinary or consultation procedure that any meeting, whatever explanation or suggestion the employee may advance, could not make any difference to the decision to dismiss.

If inadequate procedures are followed, but the result would have been the same, this will affect the employee's remedy, and could mean that no compensation is paid: it will not affect the unfairness of the dismissal. If an industrial tribunal decides that consultation might have made no difference, or in all probability would have made no difference, it is likely to reduce the compensation award made to the employee, but will still hold that the dismissal was unfair.

E.11.1   Warnings

E.11.1.1   Except for gross misconduct, dismissal should not be the sanction for a first offence. The ACAS code lays down, for minor offences, a three-stage warning process: oral warning, first written warning, final written warning and dismissal. The number of warnings may however be reduced either because of practicalities or because an offence is of a more serious nature.

E.11.1.2   Generally, an employer should give an employee a first (perhaps oral) warning for minor offences, and a written warning for more serious offences or subsequent offences.

E.11.1.3   Successive warnings need not relate to the same subject-matter.

E.11.1.4   *Lapsed warnings.* In the absence of an express provision regarding the lapsing of warnings, it is generally assumed that first warnings and non-final written warnings should lapse after six months and final warnings after 12 months.

E.11.1.5   A warning subject to appeal can still be relied upon when taking action regarding a fresh offence, though an employer must, when deciding what weight to attach to the earlier warning, bear in mind that it is subject to appeal.

E.11.1.6   Warnings are especially important where rules have recently been disregarded in practice. For example, it was unfair to dismiss a man for sleeping on a night shift where in practice his colleagues had been doing the same, to management's knowledge, for some time.

E.11.1.7   A warning will not be necessary in the following circumstances:

E.11.1.7.1   Where the employer's rules clearly spell out that a particular action will result in instant dismissal.

E.11.1.7.2   Where the employee's conduct is likely to endanger safety.

E.11.1.7.3   Where a warning would make no difference, for example because the employee refuses to accept he has done anything wrong.

E.11.1.7.4   Where the employee knew that he was putting his job in jeopardy.

E.11.2   **Investigation**

E.11.2.1   Unless the employee has been caught red-handed, the employer
             should always make proper investigation of all the circumstances.
             If necessary, he should take witness statements and examine all
             relevant documents.

E.11.2.2   Witnesses should be asked to deal with the following points:

E.11.2.2.1   The date, time and place of any observation or incident.

E.11.2.2.2   Whether the individual had an opportunity to observe clearly
               what happened.

E.11.2.2.3   The details of the event.

E.11.2.2.4   Any additional facts which have a bearing on the event.

E.11.2.2.5   Whether the individual has any reason to be biased against the
               employee.

E.11.2.3   The employer should have conduct of any investigation and
             should not rely on any parallel police investigation. It is, too,
             preferable not to have police present during any disciplinary
             meeting.

E.11.2.4   An employer should consider whether to suspend an employee
             (with pay unless the contract provides otherwise) during the
             course of any investigation.

E.11.2.5   No disciplinary action against a trade union official beyond an
             oral warning should be taken without first discussing the matter
             with a senior trade union representative or full-time official.

E.11.3   **Disciplinary meeting**

             Following internal investigation, the employer should hold a
             disciplinary meeting.

E.11.3.1   Once the employer has conducted his internal investigation he
             should ask the employee to attend a disciplinary meeting. Ideally,
             the employee should be told the following:

E.11.3.1.1   the fact that the meeting will be a disciplinary meeting;

E.11.3.1.2   the topics which will be discussed at the meeting;

E.11.3.1.3   the fact (if it be the case) that the employer is considering dismissal as a sanction;

E.11.3.1.4   the right of the employee to be accompanied by a colleague or trade union representative.

E.11.3.2   The meeting should preferably be chaired by the person who will be responsible for taking the decision to warn or dismiss. Ideally, he should conduct the meeting in the following manner, though failure to adhere to this plan will not automatically render a dismissal unfair:

E.11.3.2.1   Explain the purpose of the meeting. Outline the structure at the meeting and inform the employee and any representative that they may ask questions or make observations at any stage, and that when the employer has set out the allegations the employee will have the opportunity to respond to those allegations either by calling evidence or by argument, and to put forward any explanation or mitigating circumstances.

E.11.3.2.2   Identify those present.

E.11.3.2.3   If appropriate, arrange representation for the employee. The employee should have the opportunity to be accompanied by a colleague of his choice, or in some circumstances a trade union representative. However the employer is not obliged to allow the employee to be represented by a solicitor.

E.11.3.2.4   Inform the employee of the allegation or allegations being made.

E.11.3.2.5   Describe the evidence to the employee. If it is in writing, give him the documents (or at the very least read them to him or explain their contents in detail). If the evidence is oral, witnesses should be called or at least their evidence should be described in detail.

E.11.3.2.6   The employee and/or his representative should then have an opportunity to put the employee's case, both relating to the allegations themselves and to any facts in mitigation. *Note*: if the employee is facing criminal prosecution, the employer must not prejudice a trial but should only give the employee the opportunity to make any statement he may volunteer; no pressure should be put upon the employee to admit guilt.

E.11.3.2.7   The employee should be asked whether there is any further evidence or inquiry which he considers could help his case. A disciplinary procedure is not, however, a court of law and an employee is not entitled to cross-examine witnesses. If an employee asks for additional questions to be put to witnesses an employer would be wise to adjourn the meeting to make further enquiries, or to ensure that those questions are put to the witnesses subsequently.

E.11.3.2.8   Those hearing the disciplinary proceedings should then consider what decision to make.

E.11.4   Standard of proof

E.11.4.1   The standard of proof is a reasonable suspicion, amounting to a belief in the guilt of the employee of that misconduct at that time.

E.11.4.2   The employer must establish:

E.11.4.2.1   The fact of his belief in the guilt of the employee.

E.11.4.2.2   That the employer had in his mind reasonable grounds on which to sustain that belief.

E.11.4.2.3   That the employer had carried out an investigation which was reasonable in all the circumstances.

E.11.4.3   Where suspicion genuinely points to one or other of two employees, both may be dismissed.

E.11.5   *Sanction*: The employer must satisfy the tribunal that the sanction he has imposed is fair in all the circumstances.

E.11.6   Notification of decision

The employee, and his representative, should be notified of the employer's decision, preferably in writing, and of his right to appeal. The employer should clearly specify any time limit within which the appeal should be lodged.

E.11.7   Appeals

E.11.7.1   If possible, the appeal body should be composed of different people to those who made the decision to dismiss.

E.11.7.2   There may be no possibility of an appeal if the employee is employed by a small family company and the decision to dismiss is taken by a senior director.

E.11.7.3   Appeals may take into account additional facts learnt since the decision to dismiss (see E.5.4.3).

E.11.7.4   Appeals should be heard speedily.

E.11.7.5   If an employee fails to exercise his right of appeal an employer may be able to argue that there should be a reduction in any compensation paid because the employee has failed to mitigate his loss.

E.12   REMEDIES I: REINSTATEMENT AND RE-ENGAGEMENT

E.12.1   Reinstatement

An employee who is reinstated should be treated as if he had not been dismissed. He is restored to his old position, and treated as if he had held that position throughout the period since his dismissal. He will receive an amount equivalent to the salary and benefits he would have earnt during the intervening period. If he would, during the interim, have received additional benefits, for example a non-discretionary Christmas bonus or a pay increase, he will be deemed to benefit from this. In making any reinstatement award the tribunal must spell out the relevant terms and conditions which will apply to the employee and the date by which reinstatement is to take effect.

E.12.2   Re-engagement

An order that an employee is to be re-engaged is to the effect that he must be offered another job by the employer or associated employer. This job may be different from his original position provided it is comparable and suitable. The industrial tribunal must be specific about the nature of the job, the remuneration and any payment to which the employee will be entitled and should take into account lost salary, benefits, rights and privileges, which should be restored to the employee. The tribunal should also specify the date by which the changes must take effect. These terms are at the discretion of the tribunal. An employee will normally be awarded full pay and benefits in the interim unless he has caused or contributed to his dismissal.

E.12.3   Making reinstatement or re-engagement orders

E.12.3.1   Reinstatement or re-engagement are only ordered if the applicant so wishes.

E.12.3.2   Reinstatement or re-engagement are not ordered if clearly it would not be practicable for the employer to comply with the order. This has been held to apply:

E.12.3.2.1   If it would lead to serious industrial strife.

E.12.3.2.2   If the atmosphere at the work place has been poisoned by the employee.

E.12.3.2.3   If the employee indicates he has no trust or confidence in the employer.

E.12.3.2.4   If there is insufficient work for the employee to carry out, particularly if the employee was originally dismissed for redundancy or if redundancies have occurred since the dismissal. This ground will not assist an employer who has engaged a replacement for the employee unless *either* it was not possible for the employer to arrange for the dismissed employee's work to be done without engaging a permanent replacement, *or* that replacement was engaged after a lapse of a reasonable period from the date of dismissal during which period the employee had not said he wanted to be reinstated or re-engaged and it was no longer reasonable for the employer to arrange for the work to be done except by a permanent replacement.

E.12.3.2.5   If the employee is not fit to return.

E.12.3.3   Reinstatement and re-engagement orders are rarely made where the employee has caused or contributed to his own dismissal.

E.12.4   Consequences if an employer refuses to reinstate or re-engage

If the reinstatement or re-engagement order is made and not complied with, and the employee has not been dismissed for a reason connected with membership or activities of a trade union (as to which see E.9.5), unless the employer can show it was not reasonably practicable for him to comply with the order, the employee will receive normal compensation for unfair dismissal calculated on the normal basis plus an additional award. The additional award is normally between 13 and 26 weeks' pay, unless the dismissal resulted from unlawful discrimination under the Race Relations Act 1976, as amended or the Sex Discrimination Act 1975, in which case the award is between 26 and 52 weeks' pay. A week's pay is subject to the statutory maximum (£205 for dismissals after 1 April 1992).

E.13   **REMEDIES II: COMPENSATION**

E.13.1   **Unfair dismissal: basic award**

Compensation for unfair dismissal has two elements, a basic award and a compensatory award. The basic award is calculated in the same way as the redundancy payment (see F.9). It may be reduced in four circumstances:

E.13.1.1   Where the employee's conduct before being given notice was such that it is just and equitable so to do, whether or not the employer knew of the conduct at the time of the decision to dismiss.

E.13.1.2   Where the employee has already received a redundancy payment.

E.13.1.3   Where the employee has unreasonably refused an offer of reinstatement.

E.13.1.4   Where the employee is aged 64 on his EDT in which case the basic award is reduced by one-twelfth for each whole month during which the employee has been employed since his 64th birthday.

E.13.2   **Unfair dismissal: compensatory award**

E.13.2.1   This compensates the employee for the financial loss suffered by him as a result of the unfair dismissal, and is subject to a statutory maximum (£10,000 for dismissals since 1 April 1992). It takes into account:

E.13.2.1.1   Loss of earnings (calculated net of tax) between dismissal and the industrial tribunal hearing, subject to deduction for anything earned during the period.

E.13.2.1.2   Future loss of earnings. This is speculative. The tribunal must estimate when the employee is likely to obtain a new job and the likely wage he will then receive, calculated on the balance of probabilities (see E.13.2.3.3).

E.13.2.1.3   Loss of benefits.

E.13.2.1.4   Expenses reasonably incurred as a consequence of looking for alternative employment.

E.13.2.1.5   Loss of pensions. This calculation is normally based on the Government Actuary's Department table, available from HMSO. In essence there are two forms of pension loss: loss of pension position accrued thus far and loss of future pension opportunities.

E.13.2.1.6   Loss of employment protection rights — normally approximately £100 — because the employee will have to build up continuous service in another employment before being able to claim statutory employment rights.

E.13.2.2   There is no compensation for:

E.13.2.2.1   The manner of dismissal.

E.13.2.2.2   Pain and suffering occurred as a result of dismissal.

E.13.2.2.3   Loss of reputation.

E.13.2.2.4   Non-receipt of discretionary bonuses.

E.13.2.2.5   Non-receipt of non-contractual benefits.

E.13.2.3   *Reductions in compensatory awards.* Compensatory awards may be reduced or diminished in the following circumstances:

E.13.2.3.1   If the employee has caused or contributed to his dismissal by his own *contributory fault*. This will apply whether the conduct was discovered before or after dismissal. Contributory fault must generally be in the nature of misconduct or deliberate incompetence. The employee must have been blameworthy in some way and not just, for example, suffering from bad health. Any reduction for contributory fault is made before the application of the statutory maximum award. For example, if the tribunal decides that the individual has lost £15,000 but has contributed 25 per cent to his own dismissal, his compensatory award will be: £15,000 − 25% = £11,250. The statutory maximum will then be applied and the award will still (for dismissals occurring since 1 April 1992) be £10,000. The award will *not* be £10,000 − 25% = £7,500.

E.13.2.3.2   If employment would have ceased anyway, for example because unfair dismissal is only a result of a procedural irregularity, an award may be nil. If warning or consultation procedures might have lasted an additional, say, two weeks but the result would have been the same, the compensatory award may be only two weeks' pay.

E.13.2.3.3   The employee is under a *duty to mitigate* his loss. He should therefore take all reasonable efforts to find alternative employment. If he does not do so, this will be taken into account in reducing the award. If he does so successfully, then remuneration from the new job will be taken into account when assessing the award, from the date when the employment starts. For example, an employee at £200 per week is dismissed. Five weeks later he takes up new employment at £180 per week. The industrial tribunal hearing is in week 15 and the tribunal estimates that the pay differential will last for a further twelve weeks. The employee will receive:

(a) for the first five weeks: £200 × 5 = £1,000
(b) the next ten weeks: (£200 − £180) × 10 = £200
(c) for subsequent twelve weeks: (£200 − £180) × 12 = £240
(d) The total received will be £1,440.

If, instead of earning a new salary of £180 per week on week 5, the employee earns £210 per week from that date, his compensation will be as (a), and will be £1,000. The fact that he has more than mitigated his loss from week 5 is not taken into account in reducing pay during the unemployed period.

In general the employee need not take the first available job, but after a reasonable period will be expected to lower his sights and take up a position with lower status and/or pay. Normally the employee will not be criticised for refusing another position with an employer who has just dismissed him. Onus of proof of lack of mitigation is on the employer.

If an employee starts up a new business which earns little at the beginning, he may still be deemed to have sufficiently mitigated his loss and the tribunal will take into account the low initial earnings.

E.13.2.3.4   If an employee has received *unemployment or supplementary benefit* between the date of dismissal and the industrial tribunal hearing, the Department of Employment or DSS may recoup the payments made out of the award of compensation. This will not apply where a case has been settled out of court.

E.13.2.3.5   In general, an *ex gratia* payment or High Court award for wrongful dismissal by an employer designed to cover loss of earnings or go towards unfair dismissal compensation would be deducted from the total award. The deduction will, however, be made before the statutory maximum ceiling is imposed. For example, if a tribunal decides that the total loss is £15,000 but the employer has already paid the employee an *ex gratia* payment of £4,000, the employee will be deemed to need compensation of £11,000, and the award will still be subject to the statutory maximum (£10,000 for dismissals since 1 April 1992). The compensatory award will *not* be £10,000 less £4,000 = £6,000.

E.13.3   Damages for wrongful dismissal

E.13.3.1   In addition to any damages as specified in E.13.3.2, the employer should also pay the employee an amount equivalent to:

E.13.3.1.1   Arrears of pay to date from termination of employment.

E.13.3.1.2   Money in lieu of untaken holiday entitlement.

E.13.3.1.3   Any unpaid but justifiable expenses already incurred by the employee.

The sums paid under E.13.3.1.1 and E.13.3.1.2 are taxable, and the employer must deduct the appropriate tax and national insurance payments from the amount paid to the employee, and account to the Inland Revenue for those sums.

E.13.3.2   Damages for wrongful dismissal (save in a case where damages are only due because an appropriate disciplinary procedure was not followed) will seek to value the salary and benefits which the employee has lost if he is wrongfully dismissed without notice or money in lieu of the whole of his notice period. Currently an industrial tribunal has no power to award damages for wrongful dismissal and an action must therefore be brought in the High Court or county court.

E.13.3.3   The *calculation of the damages award* is made up as follows:

E.13.3.3.1   Net wages lost during the notice period.

E.13.3.3.2   *Plus* the net value of benefits lost during the notice period. Benefits include:

(a) Car (with or without general maintenance or petrol expenses).
(b) Share options. If an employee has share options under a scheme which provides, as most do, that the loss of options on termination of employment, howsoever caused, shall not give rise to a claim for damages for wrongful or unfair dismissal, no loss will be suffered. If no such clause exists, then one may calculate damages for lost benefit options.
(c) Pension benefits. Pension. Normally, employers' pension contributions are valued. If none is expressed, contributions are normally deemed to be 10 per cent of basic gross salary.

(d) Non-discretionary bonuses and commissions.
(e) Health insurance.
(f) Permanent health insurance.
(g) Life insurance.
(h) Free or reduced rate accommodation.
(i) Travel or goods subsidies.
(j) Payment of home telephone bills, newspaper bills, television or video rental, etc.
(k) Membership of clubs or professional bodies.

E.13.3.3.3   *Less* any social security payments received.

E.13.3.3.4   *Less* any sums received by the employee because he mitigated his loss by finding alternative employment or was unreasonable in failing to mitigate (see E.13.2.3.3).

E.13.3.3.5   *Less* any discount for accelerated payment (see E.2.3.1.2).

E.13.3.3.6   No damages will be awarded to reflect the manner of the dismissal or any pain, suffering or loss of reputation as a result of the dismissal.

E.13.3.3.7   Under sections 148 and 188 of the Income and Corporation Taxes Act 1988, the first £30,000 of any payment made upon termination of employment or loss of office is free of tax. Any payment above that level is taxed at the employee's current marginal rate. Therefore, having calculated the total sum due, if it is over £30,000 that element above £30,000 must be 'grossed up' before the final payment is arrived at.

E.13.3.4   *Note*: Before paying any director of a public company damages for wrongful dismissal, regard should be had to sections 311 to 320, Companies Act 1985, which provide that shareholder consent is from time to time necessary; whether or not the payment should be regarded as a Class 4 transaction under the rules of the Stock Exchange; and rule 21 of the City Code on Takeovers and Mergers.

E.13.3.5   If an employee recovers damages in an industrial tribunal for unfair dismissal, but those damages cannot be shown to be specifically attributable to loss of earnings for any period, the employer will not be obliged to give credit for the compensatory award received when calculating damages for wrongful dismissal. The employee will, however, be obliged to give credit for any *ex gratia* payment already received from the employer before any court action.

E.14   METHOD OF CALCULATION OF DAMAGES

Annual value *of package*	*Gross* *value*	*Taxable* *element*
Salary	a	a
Contractual benefits (as per B.13.3.3.2 (a)-(k))	b	b
Employer's pension contributions	c	—
Value of car	d	(Subject to government tables)
Total	e	f

Calculation of employee's personal allowances:
(Single person's allowance = £3,445
Married couple's allowance = £1,720 from 6.4.92)   g

Taxable pay (f-g)   h

Calculation of tax:
1.	£2,000 @ 20%	400
2.	(Up to £21,700) @ 25%	i
3.	h − £23,700 @ 40%	j
	Annual tax	k

Employee's national
insurance contributions   l
Net annual pay (e − k − l) =   m
Net loss during notice period
($\frac{1}{12}$ × m × number of months'
notice due)   n

Deductions:
1.	Discount for mitigation of loss	o
2.	Discount for accelerated payment	p
3.	Any social security payment	q

Total deductions   r
Total contractual loss (n − r) =   s

Add (if appropriate) any redundancy
payment — (see pp. 123–4)   t

Total loss (s + t)   u

Gross up (assuming marginal rate equals 40%):

$$u - £30,000 = v$$
$$v \times \frac{100}{60} = w$$

Total payment due (less any *ex gratia* payment received) $= w + £30,000$

Note: Compensation for unfair dismissal, if awarded, will be added to 't'.

E.15 PROCEDURE

E.15.1 An employee must bring an action, on Form IT1 (obtainable from any industrial tribunal), for unfair dismissal by delivering the form to the central office of the industrial tribunals within three months of the actual date of dismissal.

E.15.2 The application is sent by the industrial tribunal to the employer who has 14 days within which to respond. Short extensions to this period may be granted following written requests to the Assistant Secretary of the relevant industrial tribunal. The employer should set out any jurisdictional or factual defences, for example that the complaint has been lodged out of time, or the employee was fairly dismissed by reason of his misconduct. If the employee has alleged that he has been constructively dismissed, the employer should argue first that there was no dismissal but alternatively that if there was a dismissal it was for a specified reason which was fair: in the absence of such a plea, if the industrial tribunal decides there was a constructive dismissal, the employer will lose the opportunity to argue that the dismissal could be fair.

E.15.3 Settlement

E.15.3.1 If a complaint is settled, the employee need not account to the DSS for the return of unemployment benefit, whereas if there is a trial and an award is made the DSS will seek to recover any unemployment benefit paid.

E.15.3.2 Settlements do not prevent employees from applying to an industrial tribunal for further damages unless they have been approved by an ACAS conciliation officer or unless they can be brought within the principle of *Courage Take Home Trade Limited* v *Keys* [1986] IRLR 427. If the parties have already fairly agreed an appropriate compensation payment and it would be unjust or inequitable for the employer to pay any further sum, an industrial tribunal may not make a further award. This is likely only to apply if the employee has received more than the contractual amount due to him, or if he has received considerably more than the statutory maximum.

E.15.4   *Ex gratia* **payments**

These are normally taken into account by an industrial tribunal when deciding what compensation to award. Any such payment should, if it be the case, be expressed to include the basic award. Otherwise it may be deemed to be only the compensatory element and a tribunal can award an additional basic award even if the sums actually paid to the employee are sufficient to cover both elements. Although there is no formal payment into court mechanism in the industrial tribunal, it is possible to write a 'Calderbank letter' making an offer to settle the case 'without prejudice' on terms but reserving the right to show the letter to the tribunal after the hearing when costs are to be considered. In writing any such letter, the employer would be wise to state that if the offer is accepted the employer will agree the employee was unfairly dismissed — in the absence of such a statement the tribunal has held it is reasonable for the employee to reject an offer, even if he is subsequently awarded a lower sum by the tribunal. Normally, however, if the employee is offered less than the amount set out in the Calderbank letter, he may suffer a costs penalty.

E.15.5   **Payments into court**

In the High Court or county court, in considering the claim for wrongful dismissal, if the employer believes that a court may award the employee some but not all of his claim, but the employer will not accept this, the employer should consider making a payment into court of the amount he considers due together with appropriate interest payments.

F Redundancy

An employer in financial difficulty often needs to reduce the number of his employees. Employees who have been employed for two years or more are entitled by statute to a redundancy payment on a sliding scale, calculated in accordance with age and length of service. Many employers are more generous and pay more than the statutory sum. The problems in implementing any redundancy programme revolve around how to demonstrate that the people selected for redundancy are actually redundant and have not been selected for some unfair purpose, and the compensation to which any redundant person is entitled.

When is a person redundant

An employee is dismissed by reason of redundancy if the dismissal is attributable wholly or mainly to the fact that the employer has ceased or intends to cease to carry on the relevant business at all, or in the particular place where the employee was employed; or because the requirement of the business for employees to carry out work of a particular kind has ceased or diminished or is expected to do so. The commercial decision that the business needs fewer employees of a particular type rests with the employer, and the tribunal will generally not enquire into whether the employer was reasonable in taking that commercial decision. It is however important that at the first stage the employer thinks in terms of the number of staff he needs to maintain the business he proposes to carry on and the positions which will thereby become vacant, and does not think in terms of which individuals he no longer requires.

When a tribunal looks at the issue of redundancy it takes into consideration not only the employing company but also, in considering the question whether the employee should be offered alternative employment elsewhere, any associated companies.

When a whole business or office closes down there is rarely an issue whether an employee is redundant. If there is any question, it relates only (in a claim for unfair dismissal) to whether associated employers have appropriate alternative work for the employee.

When, however, an employer is merely reducing numbers rather than closing the business altogether, problems can arise if he cannot actually show that his cost-cutting measures are the direct cause of a particular person's departure. If he is to avoid successful claims of unfair dismissal, he must ensure that a proper method of selecting people for redundancy is implemented.

Selection of those employees to be made redundant

If an employer has a customary arrangement or agreed procedure for selection of employees for redundancy, he must adhere to that arrangement or procedure unless there are special reasons justifying a departure from it. In particular, an employer must not use as his principal reason for selecting a person any facts relating to the individual's membership of or participation in the affairs of a trade union. Any dismissal in contravention of these provisions is automatically unfair.

If there is no customary arrangement or agreed procedure, the employer must choose his own selection criteria, which must be reasonable. Most criteria include one or more of the following factors: the type of skills and capabilities for which there is a continuing employment need, and the suitability for the individuals to perform those tasks; competence; health; conduct; and last in first out. The criteria should be capable of being objectively checked, but can be weighted.

In addition, the pool from which employees are to be selected for redundancy needs to be ascertained. If, for example, an employer decides that he needs two fewer employees in one department, yet there are employees in another department who perform similar tasks and who, by their contract of employment, could be required to work in the first department, then those other employees should also be subject to the same criteria for selection. This 'bumping' rule is sound practice to follow, though it is not a hard and fast rule in every case.

Consultation

Consultation over the redundancies should take place on two levels, both the collective and the individual.

In cases where the employers recognise an independent trade union to conduct collective bargaining on behalf of a section of employees, employers should consult with the trade union as soon as possible and at least 30 days before any dismissal takes effect, where the employer proposes to dismiss as redundant between 10 and 99 employees at one establishment, and at least 90 days before any dismissal where the employer proposes to dismiss at least 100 employees. These time limits apply unless there are special circumstances which render it not reasonably practicable for them to be adhered to. Even where no trade union is recognised, employers also have to notify the Department of Employment, on form HR1, of the intention to effect redundancies, within similar time limits to those required for consultation with recognised trade unions. Failure to consult with trade unions renders the employer liable to a protective award, at the suit of the trade union itself, which amounts in essence to an extension of the notice period for each employee notionally extending the date upon which the dismissals take effect to 30 days or 90 days (as the case may be) from the date consultation first began.

At this stage, employers would be wise to see if their redundancy requirements can be satisfied by volunteers, and volunteers may be requested to come forward. Any volunteer selected for redundancy need not satisfy the relevant selection criteria. The employer is not bound to accept any volunteer for redundancy but if he fails to do so, and there is little to choose between the volunteer and the person finally selected for redundancy, the employer must be prepared to justify the reason for refusing the volunteer's application. One such reason might be that the acceptance of volunteers would detrimentally alter the balance of skills in the workforce.

Whether or not a trade union is recognised, employers have a duty to consult with each individual employee whom they propose to make redundant before any decision is finalised. This is one of the basic principles of fairness, and can only be avoided if the employer knew at the time of the dismissal for redundancy that consultation could have no effect whatsoever on the final result. It will only be in a rare case that a tribunal will hold that an employer was reasonable to form this view. A failure by the employer to warn and consult his employees will normally make any dismissal for redundancy unfair.

Alternative employment

Employers also have a duty, if someone is provisionally selected for redundancy, to see if there is any other role which might suit that particular employee, not only with the employer but also with any associated company of the employer. If this question is ignored, a dismissal is normally rendered unfair. If there are jobs, even if they are of lower status or carry lower wages than those which apply to the employee's present job, the prospect of moving to the alternative employment should nevertheless be raised.

If the employer is able to identify suitable alternative work, either within his own company or with an associated company, which is substantially similar to the employee's previous position and commands a similar wage package, it is to the employer's advantage to offer such a job to the prospectively redundant employee. The job offer, which should be made within four weeks of the termination of the redundant job, is then generally subject to a four-week trial period (though the trial period may be extended if the employee has further training). If the employee accepts the job offer and continues to work after the trial period, there is no redundancy. If, however, he refuses a suitable job offer (either immediately or during the trial period) he will lose his right to a redundancy payment unless he can show that it was reasonable for him to reject the offer. If the job is not suitable, or if the employee acts reasonably in refusing it (respectively an objective and a subjective test) the employee will still be redundant unless he accepts the job offer and continues to work normally.

Calculation of redundancy payment

The redundancy payment is set according to a fixed formula. Provided that the employee has been employed for a minimum of two years (or would have been had the statutory notice period been taken into account) the employee will receive a redundancy payment calculated by multiplying his weekly remuneration (subject to a maximum payment, which, for the year beginning 1 April 1992 is £205) by a factor determined in accordance with age and length of service.

In addition to the redundancy payment, each employee is entitled either to be asked to work out his contractual notice period, or to be paid money in lieu of notice.

F.1   **PROCEDURE FOR SELECTION OF PEOPLE FOR REDUNDANCY: GENERAL CONSIDERATIONS**

F.1.1   Are there economic or practical reasons why the employer needs to reduce his workforce? If so, he may take the decision in principle that he should make redundancies. The employer will need to explain why any redundancies are necessary, but will not be required to show that those reasons are empirically justifiable:

F.1.1.1   has the employer ceased, or does he intend to cease carrying on business, either in total or at a particular place? If yes, then all his employees or all employed at the relevant place will provisionally be redundant; or

F.1.1.2   does the employer require fewer people to do work of a particular kind, either in total or at a particular place? If yes, some of the people performing that work will provisionally be redundant.

F.1.2   The employer should establish which jobs he wishes to make redundant, and whether any job functions will in future be varied to encompass different or additional tasks.

F.1.3   The employer should consider whether there are any other options such as reduction of overtime, restrictions on recruitment, or retirement of employees which will reduce the number of those who will need to be made redundant.

F.2   **SELECTION CRITERIA**

F.2.1   Is there a customary arrangement or agreed procedure for selecting people for redundancy?

F.2.2   Are there any 'special reasons' to depart from a customary arrangement or agreed procedure? These reasons should relate to the general situation and circumstances, and cannot be used to justify selecting individuals on a personal basis. For example, an employer has 12 general haulage workers. Economic circumstances prompt him to make five redundancies. He requires all those who remain to have HGV licences, but his normal selection procedure is last in first out (LIFO). He can vary his selection criteria so that those without HGV licences can be selected first, and LIFO will apply to the remainder.

F.2.3   In the absence of a customary arrangement or agreed procedure, the employer should adopt selection criteria which can be applied objectively, and may include:

F.2.3.1   Suitability to perform the tasks that will be required.

F.2.3.2   Ability/experience/qualifications/efficiency/age.

F.2.3.3   Length of service — last in first out.

F.2.3.4   Conduct/attendance record (taking into account reasons for poor conduct or attendance).

                 These criteria may be weighted by giving some, say, marks out of five and other more important criteria marks out of ten.

F.2.4   Selection should not be on a subjective basis; for example, 'those whom the relevant managers believe are necessary to make the company viable' is too subjective.

F.2.5   The pool of employees from which selection will be made must be clearly defined. If individuals whose jobs are to go are capable of performing the work carried out by people in other departments, or can be contractually required to carry out such work (and vice versa) , serious consideration should be given to including people in those other departments in the pool for selection. This is not a hard and fast rule, but if it is to be rejected, adequate reason should be given in the event that the issue is raised in tribunal proceedings.

F.2.6   Employers should make sure that they do not select people for redundancy because of their membership of or participation in the activities of a trade union, or lack of it, or because they are pregnant, or by reason of sex or race. Such dismissals are automatically unfair.

F.2.7   Employers must be able to show they have applied the criteria objectively and reasonably. This is best done by documenting the way in which the criteria are applied.

F.3   CONSULTATION WITH TRADE UNIONS

F.3.1   Is there a recognised trade union to bargain on behalf of individuals who are members of the class who may be made redundant? If yes, the employer must consult with the union before implementing redundancies.

F.3.2   Will there be nine or fewer redundancies? If so, consultations should begin as soon as possible.

F.3.3   Will there be between 10 and 99 redundancies over a period of 30 days? If so, consultations should begin as soon as possible, but at least 30 days before the dismissal takes effect.

F.3.4   Will there be 100 or more redundancies over a period of 90 days? If so, consultations should begin as soon as possible but at least 90 days before the first dismissal takes effect.

F.3.5   Are there any special circumstances which make it not reasonably practicable for the notice set out in F.3.2, F.3.3 or F.3.4 to be given? If so, the employer's duty is still to consult as soon as possible.

F.3.6   Within the relevant time limits, the employer should disclose in writing to trade union representatives:

F.3.6.1   the reasons for his proposals;

F.3.6.2   the numbers and descriptions of employees whom it is proposed to dismiss as redundant;

F.3.6.3   the total number of employees of any such description employed by the employer at the establishment in question;

F.3.6.4   the proposed method of selecting the employees who may be dismissed; and

F.3.6.5   the proposed method of carrying out the dismissals, with due regard to any agreed procedure, including the period over which the dismissals are to take effect. (See Appendix.)

If this is not done, the trade union may apply to court for a protective award entitling redundant individuals to additional payments.

F.3.7 Consultations with union representatives should take place about the best methods of achieving the employer's objectives and, in the absence of any customary arrangement or agreed procedure relating to selection, the appropriate selection criteria to be applied and the application of the selection criteria to particular individuals. Any suggestions put forward by union representatives (for example about alternative solutions to the employer's problems or finding alternative employment) should be considered and, if not taken up, unions should be informed why their suggestions have not been accepted. (See Appendix.)

If this is not done, there may be an unfair redundancy.

F.4 NOTIFICATION TO DEPARTMENT OF EMPLOYMENT

F.4.1 Employers should, within the same periods as set out in F.3.2, F.3.3 and F.3.4, notify the Department of Employment on form HR1 of their proposals to dismiss people for redundancy.

F.4.2 A copy of form HR1 should be sent to any recognised trade union.

F.5 ALTERNATIVE EMPLOYMENT

F.5.1 Employers should find out what vacancies exist at the workplace in question or at any other workplaces within the company or its associated companies.

F.5.2 Employers should consider whether any vacancies will be suitable for any of the employees provisionally selected for redundancy.

F.5.3 Employers should consider whether the retraining of potentially redundant employees to fit any identified vacancies is a viable option and if it is, retraining should be the subject of consultation with the union or the individual.

F.5.4 Employers with large staff turnover should consider whether any vacancies are likely to arise in the near future. If they are, consideration should be given to postponing some or all of the redundancies. Any new vacancy must (if it is to be effective in negativing any redundancy) be offered before termination of employment but must commence within four weeks of that termination.

F.6   **CONSULTATION WITH INDIVIDUALS**

F.6.1   Employers should consider whether to ask for volunteers.

Any volunteer who comes forward will not need to match the
selection criteria. The employer need not accept the volunteer's
request, but should have reasonable reasons for any refusal.
People who withdraw their applications for voluntary redundancy
before their employment is terminated should no longer be
regarded as volunteers.

F.6.2   Employers should contact the individuals who may be selected for
redundancy, warning them of the situation and inviting them to
consultation.

If employees are given notice terminating their employment at or
before this stage, their redundancy is unlikely to have been fair,
unless the employer can show he knew at the time that any
consultation was bound to have absolutely no effect on the result,
and be utterly useless.

F.6.3   During consultation with individuals, employers should explain
the selection criteria to each individual, and state why the
individual has provisionally been selected in accordance with
those criteria. The employer should inform the employee, to the
extent known, of the likely amount and make-up of any termination payment.

F.6.4   The employer should explain to the employee what alternative
jobs are available.

If they are suitable for the individual (for example they do not
involve dissimilar status, pay or location) the employee should be
offered the job, subject to a trial period of at least four weeks if the
new job is not identical to the individual's previous one.

If an alternative position is too dissimilar to be regarded as a
suitable alternative for the individual employee, the individual
should nevertheless be informed of the vacancy and should be
asked whether he/she wishes to be considered for it.

F.6.5   The employer should ask the individual if there are any other
job(s) for which the individual would like to be considered and
discuss the individual's suitability for such job(s).

F.6.6   The employer should ask the individual for comments and
observations, for example on the applicability of the selection

criteria to the individual, or on the availability of alternative employment.

F.6.7   The employer should explain that anyone made redundant will be allowed reasonable time off to seek alternative employment.

F.7   MAKING THE DECISION

F.7.1   The employer should decide, after consideration of all representations made, how many redundancies should be effected and who is to be selected for redundancy.

F.7.2   It is advisable for the employer to consider offering individuals alternative employment, if appropriate.

If suitable alternative employment is offered before the employee's employment terminates, to start within four weeks of the termination date, there will normally be no entitlement to a redundancy payment unless the employee reasonably refuses the alternative offer, either before or after a four-week trial period. Grounds for reasonable refusal include:

F.7.2.1   The new job is much further away from home than the old one, and travel arrangements are more difficult.

F.7.2.2   The new job involves different hours of work, which do not fit in with the employee's other commitments (for example, the new hours make it more difficult to arrange appropriate childcare).

F.7.2.3   The new job involves working in conditions which exacerbate a particular health problem of the employee.

F.7.3   The employer should give notice to individuals, terminating their employment, either requiring them to work out their notice or paying them money in lieu of notice.

F.7.4   If a vacancy arises while employees are on notice, that vacancy should be offered to a suitable employee who was the last in the relevant category to be selected for redundancy.

F.8   ENTITLEMENT TO A REDUNDANCY PAYMENT

An individual is not entitled to a redundancy payment if:

F.8.1   He is not an employee of the relevant company.

F.8.2   He is over 65 or under 18 years old.

F.8.3   He has been continuously employed by the employer for less than two years (including any statutory notice period due) and worked 16 hours or more per week. (For continuity of employment see E.3.2.)

F.8.4   He has been continuously employed for less than five years (including any statutory notice period due) and has worked between 8 or more and less than 16 hours per week. (For continuity of employment see E.3.2.)

F.8.5   He has been dismissed by reason of misconduct before the employment terminates (provided that, if any notice is given or if any payment in lieu of notice is made, it is accompanied by a statement that the misconduct is so serious the employer would be entitled summarily to terminate the employment).

F.8.6   He is participating in industrial action at the date of termination of employment.

F.8.7   He has accepted alternative employment offered before the employment terminated either by the employer or by an associated company of the employer, and has continued in that employment after any trial period has ended.

F.8.8   He has unreasonably refused suitable alternative employment offered before the termination of employment and begun or to begin within four weeks of the termination date, either with the employer or with an associated company of the employer.

F.8.9   He has left the employer before the termination date is fixed.

F.8.10   He has resigned during his notice period, and the employer has required him to withdraw the notice and has warned that if he leaves the employer will contest entitlement to a redundancy payment (note in these circumstances, some redundancy payment may be due).

F.8.11   He is entitled, within one week of the termination date, to receive a secure pension of at least one-third of his annual pay.

F.8.12   He is abroad at the date of dismissal (unless he ordinarily worked in Great Britain in the sense that his work base was in Great Britain).

F.8.13   He normally worked abroad (unless on the termination date he is in Great Britain on the instructions of his employer).

F.8.14   He is employed by an overseas government.

F.8.15   He is a Crown servant, member of the armed forces, share fisherman, or domestic servant where the employer is a close relation.

F.8.16   He is on a fixed-term contract of at least two years' duration which specifies that no redundancy payment will be made, and which terminates because it has come to the end of the fixed term.

F.9   **AMOUNT OF REDUNDANCY PAYMENT**

F.9.1   Calculate the gross pay an employee is contractually entitled to receive for the normal working week, including the value or proportionate value of any bonus, allowance or commission if they are non-discretionary.

F.9.1.1   For time workers, multiply the hourly rate by the normal number of hours worked.

F.9.1.2   For 'piece' workers, multiply the normal number of hours worked by the average hourly rate of remuneration over the 12 weeks before the termination date (excluding weeks when no remuneration was earnt).

F.9.1.3   For shift or rota workers, multiply the average number of hours worked by the average hourly rate of remuneration over the 12 weeks before the termination date (excluding any weeks when no remuneration was earnt).

F.9.2   Calculate the length of service, adding on statutory notice periods if employment was terminated without notice.

F.9.2.1   Include any period of employment with a previous employer if the identity of the employer changed as a result of a transfer of undertaking or the previous employers were associated employers.

F.9.2.2   Anyone on maternity leave should be treated as having been employed until her notified date of return.

F.9.3   Work out the appropriate redundancy payment by multiplying one week's gross pay (subject to the statutory maximum which, for the year beginning 1 April 1992, is £205) by a factor depending upon age and number of completed years of service:

F.9.3.1   for every year during the whole of which the employee was aged 41 or over – $1\frac{1}{2}$;

F.9.3.2   for every year during the whole of which the employee was aged between 22 and 40 – 1;

F.9.3.3   for every year during the whole of which the employee was aged between 18 and 21 – $\frac{1}{2}$;

subject to a reduction for those aged 64 of one-twelfth for every month since the employee's 64th birthday. The multipliers are set out in the Ready Reckoner produced by the Department of Employment for calculating the number of weeks' pay due to employees as a redundancy payment, which is reproduced in the Appendix to this chapter, on pp. 123–4 by kind permission of HM Government.

F.10   **PRACTICAL ARRANGEMENTS**

F.10.1   The employer should give the employee a statement showing how the redundancy payment has been calculated.

F.10.2   The employer should calculate any money due to the employee in lieu of notice, which may be paid gross or net.

F.10.3   The employer should pay the employee the payments due. Payments made of £30,000 or less will generally be free of tax. It is wise for the employer to retain a receipt from the employee and to seek the employee's acknowledgement that the sums are paid in settlement of all claims the employee may have against the employer.

F.10.4   If the employer is insolvent, the Government will pay:

F.10.4.1   Up to eight weeks' wages for each individual (up to a maximum of £205 per week).

F.10.4.2   Pay during statutory notice period (subject to a maximum of £205 per week).

F.10.4.3   Up to six weeks' pay in lieu of holiday entitlement (up to £205 per week).

F.10.4.4   Any basic award due following an unfair dismissal claim.

F.10.4.5   Reimbursement of apprenticeship fees.

F.10.4.6   Payment of any unpaid pension contribution.

F.11   **APPENDIX: READY RECKONER FOR CALCULATING THE NUMBER OF WEEKS' PAY DUE**

To use the table:

F.11.1   Read off employee's age and number of complete years' service. The table will then show how many weeks' pay the employee is entitled to. (The table starts at 20 because no one below this age can qualify for a redundancy payment — service before the employee reached the age of 18 does not count.)

F.11.2   For employees aged between 64 and 65, the cash amount due is to be reduced by one-twelfth for every complete month by which the age exceeds 64.

Service (years)	2	3	4	5	6	7	8	9	19	11	12	13	14	15	16	17	18	19	20
Age (years)																			
20	1	1	1	1	—														
21	1	1½	1½	1½	1½	—													
22	1	1½	2	2	2	2	—												
23	1½	2	2½	3	3	3	3	—											
24	2	2½	3	3½	4	4	4	4	—										
25	2	3	3½	4	4½	5	5	5	5	—									
26	2	3	4	4½	5	5½	6	6	6	6	—								
27	2	3	4	5	5½	6	6½	7	7	7	7	—							
28	2	3	4	5	6	6½	7	7½	8	8	8	8	—						
29	2	3	4	5	6	7	7½	8	8½	9	9	9	9	—					
30	2	3	4	5	6	7	8	8½	9	9½	10	10	10	10	—				
31	2	3	4	5	6	7	8	9	9½	10	10½	11	11	11	11	—			
32	2	3	4	5	6	7	8	9	10	10½	11	11½	12	12	12	12	—		
33	2	3	4	5	6	7	8	9	10	11	11½	12	12½	13	13	13	13	—	
34	2	3	4	5	6	7	8	9	10	11	12	12½	13	13½	14	14	14	14	—

Service (years)	2	3	4	5	6	7	8	9	19	11	12	13	14	15	16	17	18	19	20
Age (years)																			
35	2	3	4	5	6	7	8	9	10	11	12	13	$13\frac12$	14	$14\frac12$	15	15	15	15
36	2	3	4	5	6	7	8	9	10	11	12	13	14	$14\frac12$	15	$15\frac12$	16	16	16
37	2	3	4	5	6	7	8	9	10	11	12	13	14	15	$15\frac12$	16	$16\frac12$	17	17
38	2	3	4	5	6	7	8	9	10	11	12	13	14	15	16	$16\frac12$	17	$17\frac12$	18
39	2	3	4	5	6	7	8	9	10	11	12	13	14	15	16	17	$17\frac12$	18	$18\frac12$
40	2	3	4	5	6	7	8	9	10	11	12	13	14	15	16	17	18	$18\frac12$	19
41	2	3	4	5	6	7	8	9	10	11	12	13	14	15	16	17	18	19	$19\frac12$
42	$2\frac12$	$3\frac12$	$4\frac12$	$5\frac12$	$6\frac12$	$7\frac12$	$8\frac12$	$9\frac12$	$10\frac12$	$11\frac12$	$12\frac12$	$13\frac12$	$14\frac12$	$15\frac12$	$16\frac12$	$17\frac12$	$18\frac12$	$19\frac12$	$20\frac12$
43	3	4	5	6	7	8	9	10	11	12	13	14	15	16	17	18	19	20	21
44	3	$4\frac12$	$5\frac12$	$6\frac12$	$7\frac12$	$8\frac12$	$9\frac12$	$10\frac12$	$11\frac12$	$12\frac12$	$13\frac12$	$14\frac12$	$15\frac12$	$16\frac12$	$17\frac12$	$18\frac12$	$19\frac12$	$20\frac12$	$21\frac12$
45	3	$4\frac12$	6	7	8	9	10	11	12	13	14	15	16	17	18	19	20	21	22
46	3	$4\frac12$	6	$7\frac12$	$8\frac12$	$9\frac12$	$10\frac12$	$11\frac12$	$12\frac12$	$13\frac12$	$14\frac12$	$15\frac12$	$16\frac12$	$17\frac12$	$18\frac12$	$19\frac12$	$20\frac12$	$21\frac12$	$22\frac12$
47	3	$4\frac12$	6	$7\frac12$	9	10	11	12	13	14	15	16	17	18	19	20	21	22	23
48	3	$4\frac12$	6	$7\frac12$	9	$10\frac12$	$11\frac12$	$12\frac12$	$13\frac12$	$14\frac12$	$15\frac12$	$16\frac12$	$17\frac12$	$18\frac12$	$19\frac12$	$20\frac12$	$21\frac12$	$22\frac12$	$23\frac12$
49	3	$4\frac12$	6	$7\frac12$	9	$10\frac12$	12	13	14	15	16	17	18	19	20	21	22	23	24
50	3	$4\frac12$	6	$7\frac12$	9	$10\frac12$	12	$13\frac12$	$14\frac12$	$15\frac12$	$16\frac12$	$17\frac12$	$18\frac12$	$19\frac12$	$20\frac12$	$21\frac12$	$22\frac12$	$23\frac12$	$24\frac12$
51	3	$4\frac12$	6	$7\frac12$	9	$10\frac12$	12	$13\frac12$	15	16	17	18	19	20	21	22	23	24	25
52	3	$4\frac12$	6	$7\frac12$	9	$10\frac12$	12	$13\frac12$	15	$16\frac12$	$17\frac12$	$18\frac12$	$19\frac12$	$20\frac12$	$21\frac12$	$22\frac12$	$23\frac12$	$24\frac12$	$25\frac12$
53	3	$4\frac12$	6	$7\frac12$	9	$10\frac12$	12	$13\frac12$	15	$16\frac12$	18	19	20	21	22	23	24	25	26
54	3	$4\frac12$	6	$7\frac12$	9	$10\frac12$	12	$13\frac12$	15	$16\frac12$	18	$19\frac12$	$20\frac12$	$21\frac12$	$22\frac12$	$23\frac12$	$24\frac12$	$25\frac12$	$26\frac12$
55	3	$4\frac12$	6	$7\frac12$	9	$10\frac12$	12	$13\frac12$	15	$16\frac12$	18	$19\frac12$	21	22	23	24	25	26	27
56	3	$4\frac12$	6	$7\frac12$	9	$10\frac12$	12	$13\frac12$	15	$16\frac12$	18	$19\frac12$	21	$22\frac12$	$23\frac12$	$24\frac12$	$25\frac12$	$26\frac12$	$27\frac12$
57	3	$4\frac12$	6	$7\frac12$	9	$10\frac12$	12	$13\frac12$	15	$16\frac12$	18	$19\frac12$	21	$22\frac12$	24	25	26	27	28
58	3	$4\frac12$	6	$7\frac12$	9	$10\frac12$	12	$13\frac12$	15	$16\frac12$	18	$19\frac12$	21	$22\frac12$	24	$25\frac12$	$26\frac12$	$27\frac12$	$28\frac12$
59	3	$4\frac12$	6	$7\frac12$	9	$10\frac12$	12	$13\frac12$	15	$16\frac12$	18	$19\frac12$	21	$22\frac12$	24	$25\frac12$	27	28	29
60	3	$4\frac12$	6	$7\frac12$	9	$10\frac12$	12	$13\frac12$	15	$16\frac12$	18	$19\frac12$	21	$22\frac12$	24	$25\frac12$	27	$28\frac12$	$29\frac12$
61	3	$4\frac12$	6	$7\frac12$	9	$10\frac12$	12	$13\frac12$	15	$16\frac12$	18	$19\frac12$	21	$22\frac12$	24	$25\frac12$	27	$28\frac12$	30
62	3	$4\frac12$	6	$7\frac12$	9	$10\frac12$	12	$13\frac12$	15	$16\frac12$	18	$19\frac12$	21	$22\frac12$	24	$25\frac12$	27	$28\frac12$	30
63	3	$4\frac12$	6	$7\frac12$	9	$10\frac12$	12	$13\frac12$	15	$16\frac12$	18	$19\frac12$	21	$22\frac12$	24	$25\frac12$	27	$28\frac12$	30
64	3	$4\frac12$	6	$7\frac12$	9	$10\frac12$	12	$13\frac12$	15	$16\frac12$	18	$19\frac12$	21	$22\frac12$	24	$25\frac12$	27	$28\frac12$	30

G Transfer of Undertakings

When a business is sold by one party to another, the Transfer of Undertakings Regulations 1981 ('Regulations'), which were implemented following the enactment of the EEC Acquired Rights Directive in 1977, operate so as to preserve, to a substantial extent, the employees' statutory and contractual employment rights which they had before the sale. In addition, Schedule 13, paragraph 17 of the Employment Protection (Consolidation) Act 1978 gives statutory continuity of employment in the event of a transfer.

The Regulations only apply to a sale of an 'undertaking' or to a part of an undertaking. They do not apply to sales of shares in a company, nor to asset sales only. An undertaking is not expressly defined, except that it is a business in the nature of a commercial venture which is a going concern, and which is situated in the United Kingdom. It is only when such an undertaking is transferred that the Regulations apply.

In addition, the rights only apply to people who are employed, under a contract of employment or apprenticeship, by the transferor *immediately before* the transfer. It is still undecided whether the transfer takes place on exchange of contracts or completion, but the better view is that it takes place on completion.

It used to be thought that 'immediately before the transfer' would be interpreted strictly and literally. However, it is now given a wider definition so that not only employees who are employed immediately before the transfer takes place are included, but also all those who would have been so employed had they not been unfairly dismissed prior to and as a result of the transfer. They are deemed to have their contracts of employment transferred.

The only exception to the normal rule about when a transfer takes place is when a business is 'hived down' by a receiver or liquidator of a company, who may transfer a viable part of the business to a wholly-owned subsidiary in the hope of making that part of the business more saleable to others. In those circumstances, the Regulations do not apply on the *initial* transfer, but only come into effect on the date when the subsidiary ceases to be wholly-owned by the parent company, or when the business of the subsidiary is transferred to another company outside the parent group.

When a business is transferred as a going concern, the Regulations provide that the purchaser of the business takes over all the vendor's rights, powers, duties and liabilities under the employment contracts; that after a transfer, any wrongful act committed by the transferor is deemed to have been done by the transferee, and similarly any breach of duty on the part of the employee before a transfer is deemed to have been a breach of duty to the transferee. For example, if the transferor has failed to pay wages to an employee, that employee may, after the transfer, bring proceedings against the transferee for recovery of the wages. On the other hand, any warnings for misconduct or incapability that may have been given by the transferor before a relevant transfer, can be taken into account by the transferee in any post-transfer disciplinary proceedings.

All aspects of the employee's contract of employment are transferred save one: the rights concerning occupational pension schemes are specifically excluded from any transfer, although it is open to doubt whether this exception is valid under the relevant European Directive.

Any employee, whether or not he was employed by the transferor or transferee, who is dismissed as a result of a transfer is deemed to have been automatically unfairly dismissed. The only exception to this rule is if the dismissal is a result of some economic, technical or organisational reason entailing changes in the workforce of either the transferor or the transferee. The reason may apply either before or after the relevant transfer. The test is a stringent one and the reason must thus be connected with the conduct or running of the business. Dismissals carried out by the transferor at the insistence of the transferee, or dismissals whose main purpose is to raise the sale price of the business, would not have sufficient economic reason to justify fair termination of employment. Even if sufficient economic, technical or organisational reasons do exist, the employer must still act fairly towards the employee and must follow all the appropriate procedures, similar to those applying on a redundancy (see F.6).

Transferred employees have one further right, that their terms and conditions of employment should remain the same following the transfer. Therefore, if a transferee seeks to change the employees' terms and conditions of employment, for example to bring them into line with those of his existing employees, any substantial change will be a fundamental breach of contract which the employees may be able to accept and claim constructive dismissal: such a dismissal would, unless the employer can convince an industrial tribunal that economic, technical or organisational reasons apply, automatically be unfair. The relevant employee must as usual have worked for at least two years working 16 hours or more per week, or at least five years working eight hours or more per week, before he could bring proceedings for unfair dismissal.

Trade unions

The Regulations also operate to transfer over any recognition agreement or other collective agreement between the transferor and a recognised independent trade union. This provision is only likely to have real teeth where the collective agreement is expressed to be legally binding, which is very unusual. If the agreement is not legally binding, either party may break it to the extent that sections of it are not incorporated into the individuals' contracts of employment (as to which see A.2.3), without fear of legal sanction.

Further, if recognised trade unions exist who have any members who may be affected by a transfer, they have a right to be notified of the impending transfer and, if measures may be taken which could affect their employees, they also have limited consultation rights.

G.1 APPLICATION OF THE REGULATIONS

G.1.1 The Transfer of Undertakings Regulations do *not* apply in the following circumstances:

G.1.1.1 When the undertaking is not in the United Kingdom.

G.1.1.2 When the sale is by way of transfer of shares in a company so that the only change is the identity of the shareholders and not the identity of the employing company.

G.1.1.3 When the sale is a sale of assets only.

G.1.1.4 When there is a *de facto* assumption of control of a business without an actual transfer of it.

G.1.1.5 Where the undertaking is not in the nature of a commercial enterprise. (See Appendix.)

G.1.2 The Regulations apply when the entity sold is a trade, business or undertaking. The Regulations do not apply to non-profit making organisations such as most charities or public bodies which do not trade. The issue is one of fact, but there is no set pattern. The entity must be capable of being run commercially, even if it is not run as a profit-making concern before the transfer (see Appendix). For example, provision of subsidised canteen services to employees, when sub-contracted out by the employer to a catering company, is generally subject to the Regulations. Finally, the entity should be transferred as a going concern. Factors which indicate that a commercial venture is being transferred are one or more of the following:

G.1.2.1   Transfer of goodwill.

G.1.2.2   Transfer of contracts with customers.

G.1.2.3   Transfer of contracts with suppliers.

G.1.2.4   Transfer of stock.

G.1.2.5   Transfer of work in progress.

G.1.2.6   Transfer of trade debts.

G.1.2.7   Transfer of trading name and trademarks.

G.1.2.8   Transfer of copyright, patents and know-how.

G.1.2.9   Continuation of identity of senior managers of the entity after the transfer.

G.1.2.10   An undertaking on the part of the transferor not to compete.

The most important single element is the transfer of goodwill, although its absence will not necessarily be fatal to a transfer of undertaking taking place. The more factors set out above which exist in a particular case, the more likely a court or tribunal is to infer that a transfer of undertaking has taken place. Each case is decided on its own facts. Transfers of franchises, farms and licensed premises can, even though they may involve an apparent transfer of assets only on, for example, the termination of a lease, amount to a transfer of undertaking where the business remains a going concern. A transfer of a business without employees, or a transfer of staff into or from a service company without anything more, is unlikely to constitute a transfer of undertaking.

G.1.3   The date of the relevant transfer is likely to be the date of completion of sale, rather than the date of exchange of contracts.

G.2   TO WHOM DO THE REGULATIONS APPLY?

G.2.1   Is the relevant individual employed under a contract of service or of apprenticeship? If not, and the individual is self-employed or otherwise employed under a contract for services, the Regulations will not apply.

G.2.2   Was the employee employed immediately before (i.e. before serious negotiations began between the parties leading to the transfer) the relevant transfer took place? If so, the Regulations will apply.

G.2.3 Was the employee unfairly dismissed prior to the transfer, for a reason connected with the transfer? If so, the Regulations will apply and the individual's contract of employment will be deemed to be transferred to the transferee of the business. The employee may bring proceedings against the transferee for reinstatement or for compensation for unfair dismissal.

G.2.4 Was the employee dismissed prior to the transfer for some reason unconnected with the transfer, whether or not that reason is ultimately valid, such as misconduct? If so, the Regulations do not apply and the employee's only remedy is against the transferor.

G.3 'HIVING DOWN'

G.3.1 Has the receiver or liquidator of a company transferred part of the business to a wholly-owned subsidiary, which remains wholly-owned? If so, the Regulations do not apply.

G.3.2 Has the subsidiary ceased to be wholly-owned by its parent, for example because of a share or asset sale (whether of some or all of the subsidiary) or because the business of the subsidiary is transferred to a third party? If so, the Regulations will apply and there will be deemed to have been a transfer of undertaking from the parent to the subsidiary company at the time when the relevant sale or transfer to a third party takes place.

G.4 EFFECT OF THE TRANSFER

G.4.1 General position

The transferee takes over all the transferor's obligations, rights, powers and duties under the employment contracts but not the obligation to consult over redundancy rights nor to assume liabilities under occupational pension schemes nor any criminal liability. Thus for example:

G.4.1.1 If the transferor fails to pay the employee's wages, the employee can sue the transferee to recover the underpayment.

G.4.1.2 If the transferor dismissed the employee before the transfer, for a reason connected with the transfer, the employee can claim reinstatement or compensation for unfair dismissal from the transferee.

G.4.1.3   If the employee has committed acts of misconduct for which he has or has not been given warnings, or if he has been given warnings for incapability, the transferee may rely upon such misconduct or warnings when considering subsequent stages in any disciplinary procedure affecting that employee.

G.4.1.4   The rule applies to both express and implied contractual provisions. A customary arrangement or agreed procedure for selection of employees for redundancy would be deemed to be carried over.

G.4.2   Continuous employment

Employees are generally deemed to have continuous employment so far as their statutory and contractual employment rights are concerned. These will include the right not to be unfairly dismissed, the right to redundancy or statutory maternity payments, and maternity rights.

G.4.3   Unfair dismissal

G.4.3.1   Has an employee with two years' or more continuous employment (working 16 or more hours per week) or five years' or more continuous employment (working eight hours or more per week) been dismissed in circumstances where the transfer or a reason connected with the transfer is the principal or only reason for dismissal? If so, the dismissal will be automatically unfair. The employee will be able to bring proceedings in an industrial tribunal against the transferee for reinstatement, re-engagement or for compensation for unfair dismissal, unless the circumstances set out in G.4.3.2 apply.

G.4.3.2   Is there an economic, technical or organisational reason entailing changes in the workforce of either the transferor or the transferee, either before or after the transfer?

If such a reason, which must be connected with the conduct or running of the business, exists, there may be 'some other substantial reason' justifying dismissal which would render the dismissal fair. Save where employees are genuinely redundant (when they are entitled to redundancy payments) such reasons rarely exist. The employer must still then comply with proper dismissal procedures (see F.2 to F.7).

G.4.4   Post-transfer variations to contracts

The transferee cannot impose, without the employees' consent, substantial and detrimental changes to the employees' working conditions, unless there is an economic, technical or organisational reason entailing a change in the workforce justifying the change (for example requiring a reduction of the workforce, or a requirement that employees need to perform very different job functions).

Any such alteration, even if it is only made to harmonise the transferred employees' contractual position with those of the employer's existing employees, is a breach of contract. The employee may resign and claim constructive dismissal. Such a dismissal will automatically be unfair unless an economic, technical or organizational reason can be shown to exist, and will entitle the employee to reinstatement, re-engagement or compensation provided the employee meets the appropriate length of service requirements, and is not otherwise excluded from such a claim.

G.4.5 Collective agreements

If the transferor had any collective agreement with a recognised independent trade union, the transfer has the effect of making the transferee (instead of the transferor) the employer party to the collective agreements. Unless the agreement is expressed to be binding, the transferee may terminate the agreement. Those parts of any collective agreement which are incorporated into individuals' contracts of employment will, however, still be deemed to be incorporated under the new regime. The agreement will only apply, in any event, if the transferred unit maintains a separate identity and is not merged into the transferee's general operation.

G.4.6 Non-transferred rights

The following rights are not transferred on a transfer of undertaking:

G.4.6.1 Employees' rights relating to occupational pension schemes (although there is one case at tribunal level to the contrary).

G.4.6.2 Rights of a recognised trade union to claim a 'protective award' against the transferor following a failure to consult the union before any proposed redundancy.

G.4.7 Genuine redundancies

Employees whose positions are genuinely redundant as a result of a transfer of undertaking may normally be made redundant and receive only the appropriate redundancy payments provided that the appropriate selection and consultation procedures are complied with (see F.2 to F.7).

G.5   **CONSULTATION WITH UNIONS**

G.5.1   **Application**

G.5.1.1   Is any independent trade union recognised for the purposes of
                    collective bargaining? and

G.5.1.2   Are any members of the union likely to be affected by the transfer
                    or by measures (such as relocation, or redundancies for those not
                    being transferred) connected with the transfer.

                    If the answer to both these questions is yes, the transferor must
                    notify the trade union of the proposed transfer.

G.5.2   **Information which the transferee must give to the transferor**

                    The transferee must give the transferor information regarding any
                    measures which he proposes to take which may affect any of the
                    trade union's members in time for the transferor to notify the trade
                    unions of those measures.

G.5.3   **Notification**

                    The transferor must inform trade union representatives, long
                    enough before the transfer to enable consultation to begin, of the
                    following matters:

G.5.3.1   The fact that the transfer is to take place.

G.5.3.2   The approximate date for the proposed transfer.

G.5.3.3   The reason for the proposed transfer.

G.5.3.4   The legal, economic and social implications of the transfer for
                    the affected employees.

G.5.3.5   Any measure which it is envisaged the transferor or the
                    transferee will take as a result of the transfer or, if no such
                    measures will be taken, that fact. 'Measure' means an action
                    which the transferor or transferee has a present plan to
                    implement, and does not include a vague idea for the future.

G.5.4   **Consultation about measures**

                    If measures are to be taken which may affect employees, any party
                    who is to take those measures must consult with the union
                    concerning those measures and consider the views expressed by

the union before reaching a final decision to implement those measures. (See Appendix.)

G.5.5 Consequences of failure to notify or consult

If the transferor fails to inform the union of the material facts, or if the union is not consulted about any measures which may be taken, the union may within three months of the transfer bring a complaint in an industrial tribunal for appropriate compensation for the failure to consult. The maximum award is two weeks' pay for the employee in question (see Appendix). The award will normally be made against the employing party in default. An award for failure to notify will normally be made against the transferor, unless the transferee failed to provide information on time regarding any measures he proposed to take as a result of the transfer or to consult about such measures.

G.6 PRACTICAL CONSIDERATIONS AND SUMMARY

G.6.1 The transferee of any business should obtain from the transferor full employment details of all employees proposed to be transferred, including in particular salary, length of service and the personnel files together with details of any contractual obligations which have not been honoured. This will enable him to value the obligations which he will be obliged to meet and carry on.

G.6.2 Both transferor and transferee should ensure that notification and, if appropriate, consultation with recognised trade unions takes place.

G.6.3 Following the transfer, the transferee should maintain records showing the terms and conditions of employment of each transferred employee. Substantial changes to those terms to the employees' detriment can only be effected by consent. In the absence of consent the employee may resign and claim constructive dismissal and a resulting claim for unfair dismissal will succeed.

G.6.4 The transferee should consider whether differing terms and conditions between transferred and existing employees will give rise to complaints under the Equal Pay Act (see B.3).

G.6.5 Neither the transferor nor the transferee may dismiss employees for a reason connected with the transfer. Such a dismissal will automatically be unfair unless paragraph G.6.6 applies.

G.6.6   The transferor and transferee should consider whether there is some economic, technical or organisational reason affecting the workforce which would justify any dismissals. If it exists, this will be an exemption to the general principle that dismissals as a result of a transfer of undertaking are automatically unfair, but redundancy payments are normally payable. Any consequent dismissal can only be effected after fair procedures have been carried out.

Appendix

The Trade Union Reform and Employment Rights Bill was published on 5 November 1992. If it is enacted in its form at the time of going to press, the material amendments to the checklists in this book are as follow:

A.4.1   The statement of terms should be given to each employee within two months of the commencement of employment.

A.4.4   The particulars contained in A.4.4.5 to A.4.4.12 must be specified as those which applied on a particular date not more than seven days before the statement is given. In addition, three further pieces of information must be set out:

A.4.4.12.A   The place(s) of work and the employer's address.

A.4.4.12.B   Any collective agreements affecting the employment, and the parties thereto.

A.4.4.12.C   Details which apply when the employee is required to work outside the UK for a period of more than one month (if appropriate).

C.1.2   Women dismissed because they are pregnant or for a reason connected with pregnancy will no longer need to have been continuously employed for any period.

C.3.1   See C.1.2 above.

C.3.3.2   In future if an employee is prevented by law from carrying out her normal duties she cannot fairly be dismissed but should be suspended on full pay (though she will not need to be paid if she has been offered suitable alternative work but has refused to perform it).

C.3.4.1   See C.1.2 above.

C.3.4.3   See C.3.3.2 above.

C.3.4.5   An employer will be obliged to provide an employee with a written statement giving particulars of the reasons for her dismissal if the employee is dismissed at any time while she is pregnant or during her maternity leave period (see below, C.4.1).

C.4.1   The Act introduces the concept of a 'maternity leave period' ('MLP'). This starts: (a) at the beginning of the eleventh week before the EWC; or (b) (if earlier) on the date of childbirth; or (c) (if later) on the first day of absence because of pregnancy/childbirth. MLP ends: (a) 14 weeks after it began; or (b) (if earlier) the date the employee is dismissed after the MLP period began; or (c) (if later) the date when the employee ceases to be under any legal restraint against returning to work.

             Provided the employee gives the employer written notice that she is pregnant, setting out the EWC or the date of childbirth (if occurred) at least 21 days before the beginning of the MLP (and, if requested so to do, produces a medical certificate setting out the EWC) or, if that is not reasonably practicable, as soon as is reasonably practicable thereafter, she will be entitled, whatever her period of continuous employment, to continue to receive all the benefits of her contract of employment, *excluding pay*, during the MLP period. In other words she will be entitled to receive any sick pay due to her during the MLP.

C.4.2   The provisions regarding MLP will override SMP provisions where MLP provisions are more generous.

C.5.1.7   The employer's request, instead of being given at least seven weeks after the beginning of the EWC or the actual birth itself, should be made not earlier than 21 days before the end of the employee's MLP.

D.2.1   The following issues will also fall to be considered:

D.2.1.4   Does the ballot paper specify the name of the independent scruitneer appointed by the trade union to report on the conduct of the ballot?

D.2.1.5   Does the ballot specify the address to which and the date by which any ballot paper is to be returned?

D.2.1.6   Is the ballot paper marked with a distinct identifying number?

D.2.4   In future ballot papers should be sent to those required to vote by post at their home addresses or any other address they have nominated, and they must be given a convenient opportunity to vote by post.

The Bill requires that a trade union must, at least seven days before the first day a voting paper is sent to any person entitled to vote, give the employer notice stating the union intends to hold a ballot, the first day when voting papers will be sent out, and a description of the employees the union reasonably believes will be entitled to vote.

At least three days before the first day when ballot papers will be sent out, the union must send the employer a sample ballot paper.

D.2.5 The Bill proposes the union should also as soon as reasonably practicable inform the employer, too, of these matters. Further, if either the employer or any person entitled to vote in the ballot requests a copy of the scrutineer's report on the conduct of the ballot, within six months from its date, the union must provide a copy of the report.

In addition, before any industrial action takes place, the union must, after the notice set out in D.2.4 and at least seven days before the start of any proposed industrial action, give the employer written notice describing the employees whom the union intends to induce to take part in industrial action, stating whether that action is to be continuous or discontinuous, and (if continuous) setting out the start date and (if discontinuous) setting out the intended dates. The union must not have induced any employee to take part in any industrial action before the commencement dates set out in this notice. A further notice must, too, be given, if any industrial action has ceased, at least seven days before it resumes, unless the action has ceased as a result of a court order or undertaking given to the court.

D.4.1 The Bill proposes that any individual in respect of whom any industrial action prevents or delays the supply of goods or services or reduces the quality of those goods or services may apply to the High Court if the action is unlawful for an injunction restraining further disruption, and may also seek financial and general assistance from the Commissioner for Protection Against Unlawful Industrial Action.

E.5.3.5 The Bill proposes that it will be automatically unfair to dismiss (a) a health and safety representative (nominated by employer or employees) on the ground that he performed or proposed to perform health and safety activities, or (b) any employee who leaves or proposes to leave dangerous parts of the work place or to take appropriate protective measures. The employee will be entitled to an additional award of damages, and in certain circumstances to interim relief. Similarly such an employee cannot be discriminated against by the employer taking action short of dismissal against him.

E.5.5.1   The Bill provides that employees dismissed while pregnant or during any maternity leave period are automatically entitled to a written statement giving particulars of the reason for their dismissal, whether or not they have been employed for two years and whether or not they have requested such a statement.

F.3.6   In addition to the other matters, the following will have to be disclosed:

F.3.6.6   The proposed method of calculating redundancy payments.

F.3.7   The Bill proposes that employees are also to consult with the unions about the ways of avoiding the dismissals, of reducing the number of employees to be dismissed and of mitigating the consequences of the dismissals. Consultation on all matters is to be undertaken with a view to reaching agreement with the trade union representatives.

G.1.1.5   The Bill proposes that the Regulations should apply whether or not the undertaking is in the nature of a commercial venture.

G.1.2   See G.1.1.5.

G.5.4   The Bill proposes that consultation must be entered into with a view to seeking the union's agreement to the measures being taken.

G.5.5   The Bill proposes that the maximum award will be *four* weeks' pay.

Index